frulTion

Creating the Ultimate Corporate Strategy for Information Technology

Chris Potts

Technics Publications
New Jersey

Published by:
Technics Publications, LLC
Post Office Box 161
Bradley Beach, NJ 07720 U.S.A.
www.technicspub.com/TakeITWithYou.htm
Edited by Carol Lehn
Cover design by Mark Brye

This book is printed on acid-free paper.

ISBN, print ed. 978-0-9771400-3-9
First Printing 2008
Printed in the United States of America

Library of Congress Control Number: 2008900003

To all the people running companies

with whom I've had the privilege to work.

Table of Contents

PREFACE

What happens when corporate strategists decide to take over the IT agenda, ignore all the IT Strategy orthodoxies and use it in ways that the IT specialists never intended? What happens to the strategy, the Chief Information Officer (CIO), the company's IT people and the investment plans for IT?

Ian discovered the answer and is about to tell us. His Chief Executive Officer (CEO) suddenly realized, with his unintended help, the true reason why the company had always struggled with IT – and that it had nothing really to do with IT.

At the time, Ian was 44 years old and the CIO of a corporation based in London, England, although he is originally from elsewhere. He'd worked hard to master the language and customs of his adoptive country.

We will be joining Ian's story just before he was suddenly faced with an unexpected choice. Did he want to become one of the corporate strategists? It was the offer of a lifetime. Quid pro quo: what would he have to give up?

Our role in the story is to observe and explore. We cannot tell Ian anything. Instead, let's see we can glean from the offer and how he handled it: about strategy and strategists, choices, passions, fears, people, language, relationships and money. I'll summarize my own observations along the way and I expect you'll have some more of your own.

Ian's story began at an off-site IT Strategy workshop in a hotel meeting room. He might have had a vague feeling that they were not doing the right thing. If so, he did not explore that feeling or build on it, and certainly did not have any alternative in mind. Not to worry (ha!) someone else very quickly figured out that alternative for him.

Ian himself is our narrator. This is his journey, in his own words.

PROLOGUE

A couple of weeks earlier
in a hotel meeting room

I should have made him write it down.

As Graham later told me, it's at moments like those that strategies win or lose. I was too busy thinking about the power failure at Windsor the day before and not paying enough attention. Graham, by the way, was our Group Strategy Director.

I heard Christine say it as clearly as anything, in a pause in the discussion. "Nobody out there values what we do." As the person responsible for our IT/Business partnerships team, she knew that better than anyone. Simon didn't hear her - or he ignored what she said. Either way, he didn't write it down, so we lost it from our List of Strategic Issues and Opportunities for the rest of the workshop. Actually, I still think he heard it as clearly as I did but maybe I'm being unfair and his mind, like my own, was somewhere else at that moment.

I do know that he heard Barry, our IT Projects Manager, say "The problem is that the business keeps changing its mind," but Simon didn't write that down either. With Barry and a number of the others, he just laughed as if we were talking about some naïve children who would finally see sense one day and sort themselves out. With hindsight, I really should have made him write that down, too, and made it the only thing we talked about and resolved before anything else.

As a result, we did the usual IT Strategy thing, focusing on technology and the people who deliver it, which – if we had just thought about it for a moment – we would have known to be too abstract, overly detailed and of little interest for most of the business executives whose strategy it was supposed to be, reinforcing why people didn't value what we did. Despite those insights from Christine and Barry, we didn't challenge ourselves to focus on more meaningful, valuable – and strategic – things.

So what did we have for me to take back to Juliette, our CEO? Worse than nothing, as it turned out. I bet myself that she would give me a hard time, which was easy because she always did. "Handbagging" as many of the male executives called it. She would get all passionate as usual, fix me with her sharp grey eyes, wave her arms around and periodically chop the air with her hands. Some said that she even got 'a real turn on' by talking about strategy, but I couldn't really say.

I had told Simon what Juliette said in my previous one-to-one with her. Simon was my IT Strategy Manager, which is why he was running the strategy workshop and why you'd think he would have been as stung by her remark as I was.

"Ian", she said looking directly at my eyes, "you and I both know that you have a good operational brain, but as far as I can see, you're still pretty hopeless at strategy. I'll tell you again - as my CIO, I expect you to be good at strategy. After four years in the job, time is beginning to run out". She was being as blunt and animated as always. While I was very careful to keep eye contact, I could see her hands gesticulating assertively in my peripheral vision.

Simon's reaction when I told him? "She obviously doesn't know what a good IT Strategy is all about. That one we did last year was our best so far. It passed the external benchmarking and Best Practice reviews with flying colors. Let's do the workshop next week. I'll put it all together and then you can go back and explain it to her. Maybe this time she'll see the light. If she doesn't, then get her to agree to those executive IT awareness workshops that we proposed in last year's strategy and they never signed up for".

I introduced Simon to Juliette once. Afterwards she said "He seemed nice enough, but I didn't understand a word he said. No, that's not true. I understood most of the individual words he used - it was the combinations of words that threw me. Are all IT strategy people like him? You obviously value him, but please keep him safely locked up in a back office somewhere. Anyway, what kind of strategist is he?"

Not being quite sure what her closing question meant, I just smiled as knowingly as I could. All I could think to say was "He's an IT strategist", and that didn't seem the sort of answer she was expecting.

Still, although Juliette would undoubtedly give me a hard time, in the end she had always left it to me to decide on the IT Strategy. I once even told her it might be better not to have one, to which she replied "Whatever you think is best, Ian. We're in your hands." As it was, I decided that it would be better to have a strategy than not, but it had been reassuring to know the extent to which Juliette trusted me to make the right decision.

So, hard time or not, I expected we would be OK.

Observations

- Robust strategies place high value on environmental feedback.
- Make sure a strategy is meaningful to its main stakeholders.
- Distinguish between operational and strategic thinking.
- Be careful not to interpret disinterest as trust.

ONE

Thursday Morning

Head office, London, England

Juliette's reaction to our IT Strategy was even harsher and more provocative than I'd expected. After the usual pleasantries she took an angle she hadn't used before.

"What the hell are we supposed to do with this? None of us have time to read seventy-eight pages of wiring diagrams, techno-speak and IT organization structures, let alone understand what it all means in practice."

"They're not wiring diagrams, they're business process maps, architecture blueprints and technology roadmaps. And anyway, the section on business strategy and processes isn't techno-speak."

"Yes, but we know all that anyway. Why do you guys insist on telling us on the one hand what we already know, and on the other what we're really not interested in? Whatever. These look like wiring diagrams to me. What is all this trying to tell me?"

I held up my copy of the Strategy. "This is our IT Strategy…."

"What is?"

"You interrupted me. I was answering your question."

"Yes, but leave out the blindingly obvious will you. I can see this is a paper about our IT Strategy, it says so on the front. I read that far. But can you please just tell me what our IT Strategy actually is?"

I thought about challenging her statement that the document she was holding, that had taken us so much work to produce, was just a paper about the Strategy. As far as I was concerned, it was the Strategy. Wisdom prevailed. Instead, I said "It's a five-year roadmap for our business processes, IT systems, IT organization, and IT sourcing, aligned with the company's business strategy."

"Why?"

"Why, what?"

"Why is our IT Strategy a five-year roadmap for our IT systems, etc, etc?"

"Because that's what IT Strategies are. It's best practice. External benchmarking endorsed last year's strategy with flying colors. And we've been getting excellent coverage in the media."

"Why is media coverage part of our IT strategy? Do you have a section on that?"

Two questions at once. I decided to answer the second one. "No, but everything we've done has been approved by Corporate Communications."

"No doubt it has, but that doesn't mean we've agreed that it's part of our strategy. So how can you align your IT roadmap for the next five years with our business strategies?"

"Well, each member of our IT Business Partnerships team sits down with their customers every quarter and gets an update on their business strategies. Our IT business analysts are involved in all the major projects. Once a year we revise the IT Strategy and re-prioritize the IT budget to make sure it's all still aligned."

"Customers?"

"Pardon?"

"You said customers. What are your people doing sitting down with our customers and talking about strategy."

"Not your customers, ours. Meaning you and the other business executives. You said we had to run IT like a business. Ok, so perhaps I should call them our partners, not customers."

"So am I your partner? Is Graham? James? Marianne? I thought you worked for me. Aren't these people your colleagues? I didn't mean you to run IT like a separate business. Why would I want you to do that? Never mind. That's probably a conversation for another day. So when you've revised the IT Strategy and reprioritized the budget, then what?"

"Then we deliver it."

"Deliver what? Each business strategy, the IT roadmap or the IT budget?"

"The IT roadmap and the IT budget. They deliver the business strategy."

"Who?"

"The business. Tom, Martin, Debbie, William….."

"So you deliver the IT roadmap and our Managing Directors deliver the business strategies?"

"Exactly."

"So what do you do when they have to change their tactics?"

"Like I just said, every quarter we…..

"I heard. But they probably have to change their tactics every day. How do you handle that? I would have expected your roadmap to be the sum total of all of theirs, evolving all the time. Surely they're the people best placed to drive our plans for IT, especially as they're the ones that pay for it all. This isn't the old days, when only you and your people knew what IT was best for us. It's the other way around now, in case you hadn't noticed. So if the businesses are not driving your roadmap, who is?"

"The company's strategic business drivers, plus the technology refresh cycle."

"That's what, not who. If we're not driving your roadmap, presumably it's the IT suppliers. That sounds like the tail wagging the dog. Anyway, enough about roadmaps. That didn't do it for me. Back to my question - so what is it? What is our IT strategy?"

"I'm sorry, Juliette, I'm not sure what you're asking me."

"I just want you to tell me in one sentence what our IT strategy is. I could tell you in one sentence what our overall Corporate Strategy is and I just want you to do the same for IT. I really don't have time to read your paper and I'm not sure I would understand it or find it interesting if I did. And I don't think I'm the only IT dummy in the Executive Team."

Seeming to realize that her passion was getting the better of her, she stopped talking for a moment then continued, "I'll tell you what, let's get Michelle to make us a coffee, I'll pop to the ladies room and give you a couple of minutes to think. I'd like to see if we can sort this out."

Juliette stood up and walked out. Almost immediately, her Personal Assistant (PA) Michelle came in, walked over to where I was sitting, stood over me and smiled. "Same as usual, Ian?" I just nodded.

About ten minutes later, Juliette came back. "Sorry I was longer than I expected. I called in to have a chat with Graham."

"That's OK. I needed the time anyway. I think I can answer your question, although it's a bit wordy. How about this: our IT strategy is to deploy technology that enables the business to create value for our customers and investors."

"Hold on while I sit down." She sat down, picked up the Strategy, held it up sideways between us, leaned forward and asked not unkindly, "Now, please show me where it says that."

"It doesn't, not in so many words, but that is what it's really all about."

"Maybe it should say it then, so we could all have a healthy debate about whether we wanted that to be our strategy and what we all need to do to achieve it. Anyway, thank you. My turn to do some thinking. Drink your coffee - how about a biscuit?"

I drank half of the coffee that Michelle had brought and ate an Orangy Crunch. Juliette always has Orangy Crunches. She's a non-executive director of the company that makes them, and a few other companies besides, but I'm sure that's not the reason she eats them and hands them out to everyone.

After an eternal minute sitting with her head lowered in thought and stroking her mouth with her right hand, Juliette briefly looked up over my shoulder and out the window, then caught my eye. "I like the bit about creating value for customers and shareholders. I don't like the bit about enabling, and I'm not sure why it bothers to mention 'the business' as if we're someone else - it's our strategy, after all. Isn't it?"

"What's wrong with enabling?"

"It's not strong enough. None of our other strategies are about enabling, they're all about delivering."

"This is about deploying IT that enables the business to create value. So it is about delivering. And the wiring diagrams - as you call them - are there to show everyone the IT we need to deliver for the strategy to be successful."

Juliette laughed, "Good try. But that's my point. Delivering, or deploying as you called it, stuff that enables us to create value for customers and shareholders is simply not enough. We have to actually deliver the value itself or our strategies aren't working."

"Our IT strategy can't do that."

"Why not?"

"Because Information Technology, on its own, delivers no value."

She paused for about three seconds. Given the speed with which she could think, that meant she had explored any number of mental connections before she spoke again.

"That's really interesting, Ian." she said, "Now I think we're getting somewhere. So traditional IT strategies are about delivering technologies that enable us to create value, but stop short of actually creating that value because IT on its own can't do that. It sounds like we - the people you keep calling the business - need another strategy that's about us creating value by exploiting the IT that people like you deliver. Or something like that. We need to make what you said our first strategic principle. What was it?" She took a red pen from her desk drawer and wrote in capitals on the front of her copy of the Strategy, speaking the words as she went, "INFORMATION TECHNOLOGY, ON ITS OWN, DELIVERS NO VALUE."

I was still contemplating her alternative strategy.

"But that's not an IT strategy, in the traditional sense."

"Well, we'll just call it something else then. Let's call it, er, our strategy for exploiting IT. Corporate. Our corporate strategy for exploiting IT. I like that." I didn't. I had a feeling I was about to become the first bit of corporate IT to be exploited.

However, this was a different Juliette. Since she had come back, she was calmer, more pensive and so far wasn't swearing. She was looking into my eyes instead of right at them; her own eyes were shining.

She appeared to suddenly switch subjects. "That IT budget you talked about prioritizing. What is it – capex, opex, P&L, cash[1]… what? I'm sorry, I ought to know this but I've not been that bothered until now."

"The IT budget is the running costs of the central IT department. Salaries, accommodations, external suppliers and so on. We capitalize as much of the project-based costs as possible and recharge everything to the business units."

1 capex = capital expenditure; opex = operating expenditure; P&L = Profit and Loss; cash = the actual money received and spent by the company.

“So it’s not everything we spend on IT as a company? What proportion of the total is it?”

“I’m sorry, I don’t know. I’m not sure what this has to do with strategy.”

“Everything.” Juliette paused, still thinking calmly at breakneck speed. “Damn, I wish I’d thought about this before. Listen. I want you to go and talk to Graham. I told him I might be sending you along when I popped out earlier. Spend some time together. Let him help you start again and come up with a better strategy than this. Then both of you come back and see me. Michelle?”

“Yes?”

“Michelle, book a two-hour session with Ian and Graham for the end of next week. Call it ‘Review of the draft Corporate Strategy for Exploiting IT’. Ian, you can tell me about your new strategy then.”

“That’s quick.”

“I think you’ll find that it gives you plenty of time to sort out the basic strategy, especially with Graham helping you. If I like it, and then the other executives like it, we can add more detail later, if we want to. Do you know, I’ve just realized something that I‘ve been wondering about IT for ages?”

“What’s that?”

"Why nobody really values what you lot do. It's time we changed that. See you next week."

Observations

- A strategy document is not the strategy.
- The language you use is taken as evidence of your mindset.
- If your company has a strategy for IT, make sure its scope covers all of the IT the company uses.
- You should be able to summarize your strategy in one meaningful sentence.
- If you have an IT roadmap, make sure it's demonstrably driven by your company's strategies and tactics – not those of your IT suppliers.
- If you run IT like a separate business, expect to be treated like one.

TWO

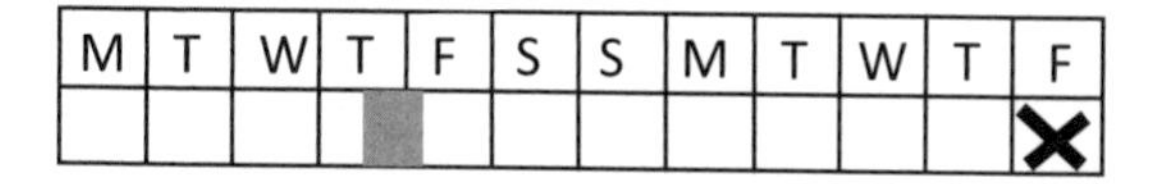

Michelle booked the meeting in Juliette's calendar, on the following Friday for Graham and me. As I came out of her office I turned left to walk past Graham's office. All the offices on the Executive floor had misted glass walls and clear glass doors to keep an element of privacy but also let natural light into the corridor and save on electricity. There were unconfirmed rumors that the glass for each office cost £10,000 (about US$ 20,000). Graham was in his room with the door open so I knocked (or kind of 'donged') on the glass wall just next to it and walked in.

"Hey, Graham, when can we get together?"

Graham was about six-foot-four, mid-forties with red hair and brown shoes. None of us knew much about him. At executive meetings he tended to hide in the shadows much of the time, but Juliette swore by him.

"Let's start tomorrow. I can do an hour and a half first thing, then I've got to go off to Whitehall." Graham was often going off to Whitehall, where many of the government offices are, for reasons that most of us were not party to.

I agreed with Graham that we would start the following morning, left his office and called Simon on his mobile phone. I wanted to give him an edited version of the session with Juliette. He asked me whether he was going to be involved in the meetings with Graham. I said no, Juliette had specifically asked Graham and me to work on this together but I would let him know how things were going. From the tone of his voice, he was obviously annoyed, but I left it at that.

I also phoned Christine. I wanted to find out why she had said almost exactly the same thing as Juliette about nobody really valuing what we do. Her phone was off, so I left her a voicemail asking her to call me back as soon as she could.

Just as I finished leaving the message for Christine, my phone vibrated and played a burst of the theme music from Mission Impossible. It was a text message from Marianne, our Group Director of Brand and Marketing. This was when text messages were still a fairly new way for executives to converse. She'd always been an early adopter and had invented her own abbreviated language. "Jlt clld. Nd to spk to u asap. Pls cll." I called, but surprisingly her phone just rang and rang until voicemail cut in, so I left her a message, wondering what Juliette had called her about that meant she needed to speak to me, ASAP.

Then I spoke to Barry. Apart from Christine, he had been the other one to speak out at our workshop only for us to ignore what he had said. I didn't have anything specific for him to do yet, but just wanted him to know what had happened and mention that Juliette had asked how we handled the business changing its tactics. In typical Barry fashion, he replied "That's nonsense. They're not changing tactics, just changing their minds. Doesn't jolly old Juliette know how hard that makes it for us?"

Ignoring the childish disrespect to Juliette, who was actually younger than Barry, I asked him, "What do you think the difference is between changing their tactics and changing their minds, and how could we accommodate the one without the other?"

"Beats me. It would be better if they just stuck to what we all agreed in the business case. All the work our business analysts, IT architects and everyone else does to put it together usually turns out to be a waste of time. Take the upgrade to APEX1 for example. Everyone's losing the point of the project and are totally depressed, the scope's changed so much."

"Please give it some thought, Barry. We may need to come up with something really quickly."

Finally, I called Lawrence, my IT Finance Manager. I asked him if we could provide the numbers for all the money the company spent on IT, not just the IT department's budget.

"Probably, but it will take a couple of days, at least, and I expect we'll have to estimate some of it. What do you need – capex or opex?"

"Both, I think."

"Depreciation? By the way, you know that's not spending, really?"

"Er, yes, let's include depreciation – better to be safe than sorry."

"Just this year's operating plan or the three-year outlook."

"Better make it the next three years, just in case."

"OK. I'll see what I can do."

"Bless you, Lawrence. Thanks. Juliette's asking for the numbers – something to do with strategy."

"You're welcome. I know what she's like."

That evening I talked my wife, Helen, through the highlights of the meeting with Juliette. Helen thought that Juliette's new interest in our IT strategy was triggered by something else, but neither of us could think what this might be. We agreed that the best thing for now was for me to go with the flow.

Next morning, I tried Marianne again on the way to work. "Hey, Ian. How're you doing? Sorry I didn't answer you yesterday. Graham came into my office just after I texted you. Juliette says that you're going to rethink the way you do IT strategy. Come and see me, I've got something I want to talk to you about." I suggested that we meet the week after next, when Graham and I had been back to see Juliette. "No way. I only want half an hour. Let's do it next week." So we agreed to meet for lunch on the following Tuesday.

Before we started our meeting Graham arranged a coffee for me and water for himself. He and I had only spoken on-and-off and never about anything deep and meaningful, so the directness of his opening question surprised me. "How much longer do you want us all to treat you like a supplier?"

"I don't want you to treat me like a supplier. Why do you think that I do?"

"Because you act like one. You talk about the business as if you are not part of it. You have people called Business Partnerships and acting like suppliers' account managers and I've heard you call the rest of us your customers. Your performance metrics are about how well you supply us with IT products and services. You've even published a catalogue of the services you provide with the prices you charge. That's why we all think that you want us to treat you like a supplier."

"But we are a kind of supplier. We supply products and services that you could get someone else to supply."

"Who's we? Some of your people do, that's true, but this is about you personally, Ian. You seem to see yourself as the 'managing director' of a quasi-supplier of IT services, with us as your only customer. Doesn't that put you in competition with the real suppliers out there?"

I didn't tell him that I'd been wondering on-and-off whether we could turn my department into a real supplier, a separate company. "Sort of. Look, Juliette wants me to revamp our IT strategy and told me to get your help. Where do we need to start?"

"We just did, but we can come at this from a different angle if you like."

The people who thought they knew Graham better than I did said that you could never quite figure out where he was coming from. Some said he played games all the time. I was already beginning to get confused by his approach to our discussion.

"I read your strategy paper last night. Juliette lent me her copy. It obviously proposes a solution to something, in considerable detail, but I can't find a clear statement or even a very strong hint of what that something is."

I told him about the 'enabling' phrase that I had settled on for Juliette.

"So the problem your strategy is promising to solve, then, is that our existing IT systems don't enable us to deliver the value of our strategies and business plans."

"Yes, that's right." Promising sounded a bit strong. Aiming, maybe.

"So if we follow your roadmap and invest in some different systems, the problem will be solved."

He said this as a statement not a question, turned to look at a large, striking picture of the Eiffel Tower at sunrise on his office wall and started to think. After a time he sat back in his chair and looked at me with an unusual, generous, expression. "Now I see why Juliette asked me to help you. When it comes to strategy, I still have a lot to learn from her."

I asked him why. As her Strategy Director I had thought it would be the other way around.

"Because this isn't really about IT at all. You need to turn the whole thing on its head."

Observations

- Don't ever underestimate the pace of corporate strategy.
- Make sure your strategy can handle people changing their minds as well as their tactics.
- Build your strategy on a promise, not an aim.
- If your strategy is founded on solving a problem, make sure that it can feasibly do so.
- Are strategists game players?

THREE

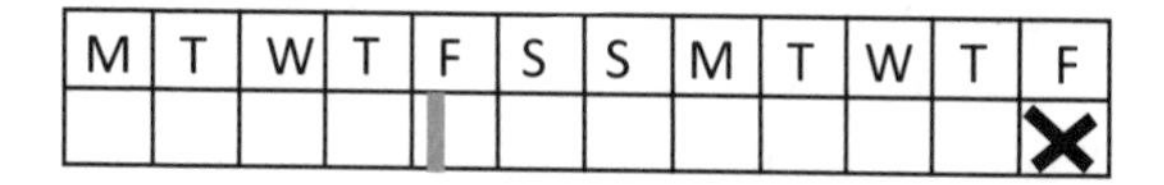

Graham, I have since realized, gets very emotional but keeps it hidden away much of the time. You don't see it in him unless you look very hard. The generous look that he gave me was because he had seen an opportunity in the IT Strategy to deal with a wider strategic problem. It was an issue that had been bugging him and Juliette for ages, but they hadn't yet found a vehicle for solving it. He was genuinely grateful to me, as fate's agent, for bringing him this opportunity and to Juliette for spotting it. He was also excited about the prospect of what lay ahead.

Far from playing games, he told me directly what the problem was that he and Juliette were trying to solve. He also told me that if I wanted to work in the 'inner circle' with them I had to stop behaving like a quasi-supplier. Suppliers do not get a say in the kind of strategy that they wanted the IT strategy to become. Why, he asked rhetorically, put myself in competition with real, external suppliers when there were things I could do as a member of the executive team that nobody outside the company would ever be allowed or able to do?

He explained that the problem we had with IT was not one of enabling, but one of exploitation. And it wasn't only an IT problem; it was just more obvious in the IT context. He reckoned that if we could solve the problem for IT we could solve it for everything, as long as we went about it the right way.

I asked him what he meant by a problem of exploitation, noticing that he was starting to use some of the same language as Juliette had the day before.

"We invest in business changes and, therefore, spend money based on business cases that promise to deliver a worthwhile return. Firstly, we're not always getting the benefits we've been promised. Secondly, we're not even sure that we have got the balance of our investments right in the first place."

"Do you mean between IT and everything else?"

"No, definitely not. I think that's part of the problem and something that you and I might need to talk to James about in the next few days." James was our Chief Financial Officer (CFO). "I'm not sure that we should have a separate plan for IT at all. It makes it too easy for everyone to talk about IT projects and the 'IT portfolio' when in reality there is no such thing. We can't create value just by spending money on IT. You, or someone else, can deliver technology that meets the requirements we've stated, on time and to budget, until the cows come home. Unless we actually do what it takes to create value from the changes we invest in, we might be better off not investing at all. What I mean by getting the balance of our investments right is making sure we invest the right proportions of our total new investment in the right kinds of value, given our strategic priorities and what we don't think we can get from the investments we've already made."

There was a lot to figure out from his last sentence. "I think I follow you. If I've got this right, the problem that you want our IT strategy to solve is about the value that people do - or don't - create from the money we invest in IT?"

"Almost. What I was trying to say, probably not very well, is that the first thing you need to do is to stop separating IT from everything else. IT is not the problem, just a symptom. The actual problem is all about money and all about people – our internal investment culture, the way we invest in business change whether or not it involves IT. Juliette and I want to solve the problem at the root of all this and we think that we can use IT as a case in point. Does that make sense?"

"In principle, yes." Well, maybe. "What did you have in mind?"

"I'm not sure yet. That's where we want you to join in and help. What do you think we should do?"

"I don't know yet, either. I'm still getting my head around it. Can I talk this through with any of my team?"

"Not if they are coming at it with a supplier mindset or just want to constrain their thinking to the IT side of things. Who wrote the strategy paper you gave to Juliette yesterday?"

"Simon Rathbone."

"Unless you really feel strongly that he should be involved, I suggest you keep him out. I don't think he's the right kind of strategist or he would have at least hinted at some of this in the first place."

"What do you mean by the right kind of strategist? How many different kinds of strategist are there?"

"OK, sorry. I always work on the basis that there are four main types of strategist. We're all a bit of a mix between them, but two types will dominate. Let me draw you a picture." Graham sketched a three-dimensional, four-cornered pyramid on his desk pad, like this:

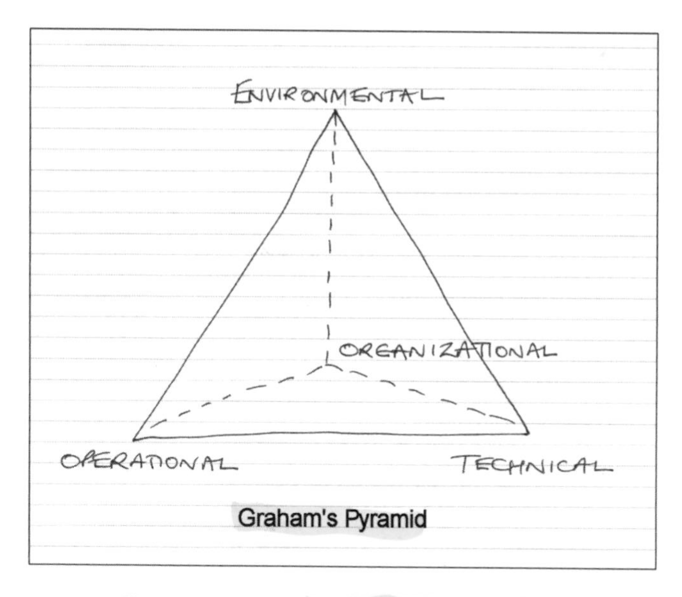

Graham's Pyramid

He explained, "There are four main types of strategic focus and we each have them in different proportions. An Environmental focus is about a strategy's external context. In business terms, this includes customers and investors and what they value, the legal and regulatory climate, the perception of our Brands and service, and the external processes that we participate in. An Operational focus is more concerned with the mechanics and execution of internal processes, production of outputs, productivity and efficiency. A Technical focus is mostly concerned with the specification of things – for example products, services, techniques and technologies. Finally, an Organizational focus is about operating models, culture, organizational structure, internal politics and sourcing."

"Why is service in there twice, both in Environmental and in Technical?"

"It isn't. Environmental includes service, because that's mainly about an experience. Technical includes services, plural, which are things you can specify and deliver. Think about a hotel, restaurant or coffee shop."

"Ah, I think I see the difference."

Graham continued, "What I've noticed more and more is that we each seem to live inside the pyramid, nearer to one side and one corner and that defines what kind of strategist we are. For example, I'm an Environmental-Organizational strategist. I focus primarily on the environment in which our strategy has to succeed and then on what we need to do differently with our culture, organization, people and politics. Strategists like me tend to rely a lot on intuition, synthesis and networks of causes-and-effects. I am not very operationally or technically minded. Something like this pyramid is about as technical as I get.

From the evidence of your IT Strategy, Simon looks like he's Technical-Operational, and probably relies more on specifications, analysis, techniques, internal process and outputs. I expect that's very common and probably very useful in the IT world, but not always much help when it comes to corporate strategy. Either or both of us would have to make big adjustments in focus if we want to have a meaningful dialogue about strategy, perhaps beyond what's humanly possibly depending upon how polarized we each are within the pyramid. That's a quick explanation. We would need a few hours to really do it justice and I'm still learning all the time. Any help?"

"Yes, thanks."

"You're welcome. Anyone else you want to include?"

"Christine Waterson."

"Who's she?"

"She's my IT Business Partnerships Manager. She has a team of people who work with the business units. She made some comments in our strategy workshop a couple of weeks ago that makes me think that she could be very helpful. Christine's definitely not a techie and is as far from being a supplier as we're likely to get."

"What kind of strategist do you think she is?"

"Er, Environmental-Technical."

"Because?"

"She thinks about the environment in which we have to succeed and then about the techniques we need to adopt."

"Excellent. You're a natural. She and I should be able to have a meaningful conversation about the strategic environment, even if our tactical focus is a bit different. OK, take her into your confidence and see what she can do to help. I'd like to meet her sometime in the next few days. I'm off to Whitehall in a few minutes, but let's see if we can agree on a Promise for your new strategy."

"What do you mean by 'a Promise'?"

Graham explained that he meant a sentence like the 'enabling' one that I had come up with for Juliette the day before. He said that a true strategist always remembers their Promise and never stops pursuing it, every moment of every day, because it's in the little moments that strategies usually win or lose.

"I'm not sure I can think of one right now", I said.

"Try this then, based on what you told me earlier. We will maximize the value we create from all the money we spend on IT."

"You've done this before."

"Absolutely, though not for IT, and that one's probably a bit too loose. If you agree to work with that as a draft Promise, please could you and Christine come and see me on Monday at four o'clock, ready to talk about why we aren't already achieving it and therefore what - in principle - we need to do."

"What about Barry Underhill?"

"What does Barry do?"

"Barry's the IT Projects Manager."

"Oh yes, I remember him now. Where does his accountability end?"

"In what sense?"

"In our end-to-end investment process, where does Barry's accountability stop? For example, is it when the IT's delivered, we've completed all the business changes we want to make, or when we've delivered the benefits of our investment?"

"When the IT's delivered and seems to be working OK."

"So he's not accountable for the delivery of value."

"No. That's the project sponsors."

"Ahhh! I wonder how the sponsors do that. Have they got their own project managers, accountable for delivering the benefits in the business case? Anyway, keep Barry briefed in confidence and pre-warn him that we may need him to provide some financial information about our projects pretty quickly, either before or after next Friday."

"OK, Monday at four – you, me and Christine. I was wondering. Why are you going to Whitehall?"

"Strategy, old boy, strategy. See you on Monday. Give me a call if you need anything."

Observations

- Being perceived as a supplier disqualifies you from making a full contribution to corporate strategy.
- If you follow Graham's Pyramid, there are 12 major types of strategist, (4 primary areas of focus x 3 secondary areas of focus).
- Different kinds of strategy need different types of strategist.
- Make sure you know your relative strengths in synthesis and analysis. Overall strategy demands a high degree of synthesis.
- Issues with creating value from IT are symptoms of a wider business problem.

FOUR

M	T	W	T	F	S	S	M	T	W	T	F
				▌							✕

Going with the flow was one thing, but having Juliette, Graham and Marianne all starting to control my schedule was beginning to bother me. I needed to start running this new agenda.

My next move was to phone Christine again. The meeting with Graham had been in our Head Office in London, but Christine was based out in Windsor, twenty miles west. She apologized for not returning my earlier call and I asked her to catch the next train and meet me as soon as she could. An hour later she phoned from her mobile to let me know that she had arrived in London and was just about to jump on the Underground. We arranged to meet in the company's staff restaurant on the eleventh floor of the head office building. It was a good place to meet and work, with a range of comfy leather armchairs and sofas, as well as the usual chairs and tables. It also has a huge floor-to-ceiling window looking out over the rooftops and the River Thames, angled outwards so that if you lean forwards you can look right down the side of the building to the street below. Some people found that the window made them nervous, so they kept well back.

While I was waiting for Christine, I phoned Barry and told him to be ready in case we needed financial information about his projects. He said it would be helpful, to say the least, if he knew what information we were thinking of and the deadline for delivering it, but I just had to tell him that I didn't know either. "Nonsense," he said, leaving me unsure whether he didn't believe me or was simply expressing his frustration at the uncertainty.

I had recruited Christine two years earlier from a retail giant. She was fed up with the 'us and them' and 'we know best' attitudes of some IT people towards the rest of the company, and the position of Business Partnerships Manager seemed to give her an opportunity to channel these frustrations in the best way possible.

We found a large, dark-blue leather sofa that faced the big window where we were unlikely to be overheard by anyone else, and sank into it. I told her about the meetings with Juliette and Graham, what they wanted from us, Graham's idea of turning the IT Strategy on its head, that Juliette wanted to call it the Corporate Strategy for Exploiting IT, and to treat it all in the strictest confidence.

"Maybe next time you'll listen to me," she said, with a smile. Christine has one of those faces that turns from plain to pretty whenever she smiles.

"We've got until Monday at four to look at Graham's Promise and go back to him with our thoughts on what needs to be done to achieve it."

Christine first response was to question the integrity of the Promise. If Juliette and Graham wanted to use IT as a case in point to solve a wider problem, why didn't they say so? A more honest Promise would be something like 'We will use our IT spending as the foundation for improving our overall performance in creating value from investments in change.' Why hide the truth?

Environmental-Technical, definitely.

I agreed that we should talk this through with Graham on Monday. He probably had his reasons. Meanwhile we would work through the Promise he had given us. If we could see that the alternative Promise would mean an entirely different strategy, then we would highlight this to Graham when we saw him, or even call him beforehand for a steer.

Christine also asked me why Simon wasn't involved. I told her, truthfully, that he would most likely find himself terribly exposed. This wasn't his kind of strategy and he had not impressed any of the senior directors who had met him so far. And I had already half told him. Was I going to tell him properly? I was still wrestling with that one.

"If it's not Simon's kind of strategy. Why is it mine?"

I took Christine through the same pyramid that Graham had shown me, and explained where I thought she fitted. She seemed really motivated to understand and use it, asked me what my profile was and without waiting for me to answer said she thought it was Operational-Environmental. Interesting. As an experiment, I suggested we both write down Barry's profile separately and then compare answers. I came up with Operational-Environmental, Christine with Operational-Organizational. At least we agreed that he was a primarily an Operational strategist. If we had more time we could have debated the second part of Barry's profile: if he was primarily an operational strategist, what did Barry next focus on tactically?

Before I forgot, I then called my PA, Karen, to tell her to clear my calendar all the way through to the end of the following week.

"You've got IBM coming over from America on Wednesday, and Oracle on Thursday. Do you want me to keep them in?"

Hell. I had really wanted to see those guys.

"No, you'd better apologies and give them both new dates in a couple of week's time."

"OK."

I remembered that Graham had mentioned getting James involved so I also called his PA and booked a meeting with him for Tuesday afternoon. Now that I felt back in control, Christine and I walked over to the counter, bought two cups of coffee and two doughnuts and sat back down in our strategy sofa.

I tore off a clean sheet of paper from my pad and wrote Graham's Promise at the top:

We will maximize the value we create from all the money we spend on IT.

I sat back in the sofa and looked over at Christine. "Graham wants us to say why they aren't achieving this already. What do you reckon?"

She sat forward, put her elbows on her knees, raised her hands to her chin, loosely entwined her fingers and looked out of the window into the distance.

"Before we do that, I think we should explore who 'we' is."

"Come again?"

"Who is the 'we' that is maximizing the value we create, and spending money on IT?"

"We, us, the company."

"But that's everybody, which can't be true. This has to be more personal. Not everybody has to maximize value nor spends money on IT."

I began to see the point of her question. The identity of the 'we' in Graham's promise was indeed a key to the strategy he had asked us to work on. I was becoming more impressed with Graham, and now with Christine, by the minute. Whoever the 'we' turned out to be were going to be the main target of this strategy and, presumably, its day-to-day owners.

"I'm not sure, Christine, but can we try this the other way around, by exception. Who isn't it?"

"No, Ian, I don't think that will work. It isn't most people. Instead, I suggest we decide whether it includes you and me, for a start."

She stopped looking out of the window, eased back into the sofa and turned to look me in the eye. She made a face with her mouth. "Well, if it doesn't include me then maybe I'm in the wrong job. I think it includes you too, but I'm not so sure about the other members of the IT Management Team. Mark, for example: does the Technical Services Manager create value and spend money on IT, or is he one of the people that the company spends its IT money on? Is the same true of Barry? Karen and Lawrence are not really in IT as such, so I'm not sure if we need to worry about them". Karen had a dotted line to me as our IT Human Resources manager, like Lawrence did for Finance. "Can I borrow your pen?"

I handed my pen to her, and she drew two large circles separately on the top sheet of my pad. She wrote inside one of them 'WE?' and the other 'NOT WE?'. In 'WE?', she put herself and me. In 'NOT WE?', she put Mark and Barry.

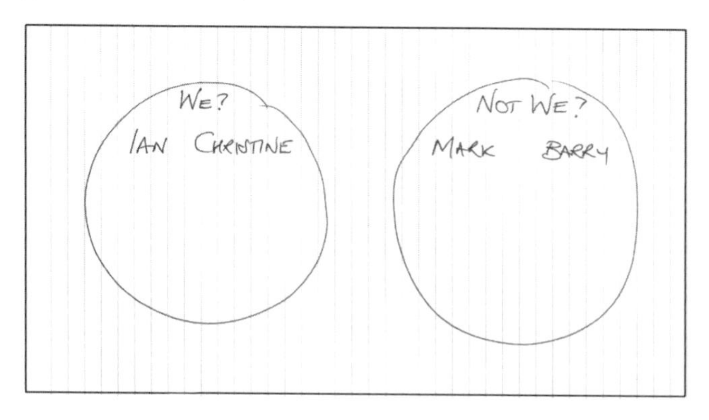

"What about Simon? Where should the IT Strategy Manager sit?" I told her that I honestly didn't know, but already we had a new picture to deal with. We had already split the IT team into two entirely separate groups.

Unhappy with this split, I suggested we overlap the circles and put people like us in the middle. "If the WE circle is the business and the NOT WE is IT, aren't they overlapping anyway – like the Venn Diagrams we learned at school? Surely we represent the overlap between business and IT?"

"But that's not what these circles are. I think the WE circle contains the customers of IT, the demand side of things, and NOT WE the supply side - or at least the people who the customers spend their IT money on. It's a different mindset. Nobody can be both WE and NOT WE at the same time."

I'd always thought everyone was divided into The Business and IT. While I was struggling with the implications of this challenge to my mental map of the world, and with it my sense of identity, I decided we should try and find more WEs and see what happened.

"I think we can safely say that Juliette, Graham and James are in WE." Christine agreed and wrote their names in the WE circle. "Are all the directors in WE? I think they must be." Christine started to write all the other directors' names in the WE circle but I stopped her. "I think we should just write 'business directors' in WE. There's no point in writing all their names if they're all going to be in there".

"No, Ian, let's carry on making it personal." She spent a couple of minutes writing all the directors' names in the WE circle, one by one. It was a bit of a squeeze, some of their names ending up quite small, but she made it.

"OK Ian, can we see what this is telling us? All these business directors, plus you and I are going to maximize the value that we create from the money we spend on IT. It looks like Mark and Barry may be the people - or at least two of them - on which we spend that money. Have I got that right?"

"That's what I think this picture tells us. Let's add IBM, Oracle, Accenture, Microsoft, and Gartner to NOT WE just to make the point."

"OK," so that's what we did. "So why are you and I in WE? What makes us so special?"

I didn't want to admit it to Christine, but I was beginning to worry more about the potential fate of me, my job and department than who else was appearing in each circle. This was all taking me in a direction that was completely at odds with the world as I saw it and where I believed I fitted in. I wanted to be in the NOT WE group, or in the non-existent overlap, but didn't feel able to say so. I had no idea what I would be doing in the WE group that was of use to anyone, separated from the familiar community people who were appearing in NOT WE. As well as turning the strategy on its head, we seemed to be doing the same for my career.

"Good question. Let's get another coffee."

Observations

- Start shaping the strategy by exploring why the company is not already achieving its Promise.
- Validate who the Promise is talking about.
- Base your strategy for IT on a model that's about customers and suppliers, not one that's about 'the business' and 'IT'.

FIVE

M	T	W	T	F	S	S	M	T	W	T	F
				▌							✕

So far, we had managed to split my IT team into two and started to question our own fundamental purpose and identity. One hell of a strategy this was turning out to be.

We drank our second coffee looking out of the window, saying nothing. Beyond the glass it had started to drizzle.

When she had finished her drink and put her cup back on the table, Christine misread the look of concern on my face and said, "Stop looking so dramatic. It's me. I'm not supposed to be on the picture. You're there because you're a business director. None of the other directors have their managers listed, so we need to take me off."

"OK, let's say we take you off, which means taking Barry and Mark off as well. Now WE includes me and all the other business directors, and NOT WE just the external suppliers. Why am I there? I'm not responsible for creating any value, am I?"

"Not on your own, maybe. But 'we' is collective. This says that you and the other directors are a team, or more likely a community, that creates maximum value from the money you all spend on IT. You need to work out your role in that community."

Without knowing it, by repeatedly talking about me and my role, Christine was stoking my worries that this was taking me in a direction I didn't want to go.

"I'd like to do that later on. Now that we have decided who is 'we' in our promise and have some examples of who isn't, let's go back to Graham's question. Why aren't they achieving the Promise already?"

We spent the next two hours talking this through, including lunch. It was a funny conversation, almost random at times. We both wrote notes and drew pictures as we went along, either to illustrate a point to each other or to brain dump for our own personal benefit. Even we couldn't make sense of much of it afterwards. In the end, we wrote the following points on a separate piece of paper:

- We don't really know how to exploit IT and maximize value
- Nobody seems to be motivated to maximize value anyway

- We don't understand the connections between spending money on IT and creating real value for customers and investors
- Business cases are used to get approval for money that people want to spend on things they want to buy
- Nobody gets rewarded or fired depending on whether a project delivers on its business case
- IT is treated as a separate investment/spending 'stream', yet on its own delivers no value
- Our IT team has an in-built conflict of interests, trying to be both a sort-of-customer and sort-of-supplier at the same time

By about 2 p.m., we were mentally exhausted and decided that was enough for one day. Both Christine and I thought that I should talk through the results of our discussions with Graham to check that were on the right track. She headed back to Windsor while I walked round to Graham's office to see if he was there. He wasn't, so I rang his mobile phone.

"I'm in the car, so I can't write anything down."

"That's OK, I only want to talk you through where Christine and I have got to today and get your feedback."

"Go ahead, what have you got so far?"

I told him about the alternative Promise, the WE/NOT WE discussions, and the bullet points we had noted down at the end. I avoided telling him that we had not worked out my own purpose yet and that I was feeling increasingly vulnerable.

"Don't worry about the alternative Promise. The circles technique sounds interesting, although I'm not quite sure I agree with your answers. There's no doubt that your WE means the customers of IT and NOT WE the suppliers, but I've realized that the Promise I gave you off the top of my head has multiple WEs, and now I think about it they may not all refer to the same group of people. That's bound to confuse. But it sounds like you're on the right track. If you think it's useful to develop that picture any more, keep going. Anything else?"

"Barry was frustrated that we can't tell him what information we're going to need, or when we're going to need it."

"OK, well I have been thinking a bit more about that. What we need is the total amount of new investment we're making in projects, categorized by the type of value those projects are promising to create. Also what impact those projects will have on our future costs to P&L."

"I expect we can get the figures for IT, if that's what you mean."

"Well, the IT figures might be useful, but I think we're going to need to know the total business investment to make any meaningful strategic decisions. The IT figures are only part of the story and presumably add up to a random number depending on how much each project wants to invest in IT from its total budget."

I wasn't sure about Graham's random number theory, but knew we were not accounting for all the non-IT investments. Also, that the project budgets tended to be set as IT-plus-anything-else, not a total budget for investing in change of which IT was just one variable element. "What if we only know the IT figures?"

"Then at least let's see what they are and leave an empty column for the overall business investment. Hey, that could provoke some debate!" His emotions were beginning to show through again.

"And those types of value you mentioned, do you have a list of what they are?"

"No, but I might have a stab next week. Meanwhile just ask Barry to do this bottom-up. See what types of value his projects are promising and use that to do the first cut."

"For example?"

"Er, protecting and growing revenue, controlling and reducing costs, Brand reputation, legal and regulatory compliance. Those are a few examples and I'm sure we'll find some more. Mind you, if we get too many we'll need to boil them down a bit."

"How many would be too many?"

"More than about ten or maybe twelve, I suppose. Is all of this any help?"

"Yes, thanks. I'll pass it on to Barry. By the way, have you met him?"

"Yes, at your departmental conference last year and in a few project steering boards I've been to. The two things I remember about him are that he's suitably passionate about what he does and that he keeps saying 'nonsense'."

"That's Barry. He can be a bit of a boy at times, but he's excellent at getting projects delivered."

"OK. Tell him we need the figures delivered by Monday morning. Have we finished?"

"Yes, that's enough for now. Thank you."

"One last thing - have you been thinking about your own role, if you're not going to be a supplier anymore? The work that Christine and you did today put you in the WE group, so that means you're going to be one of us at last." It was a statement, not a question. "Where, in our new world, do you fit in - assuming that you do?"

Not wanting to deal with that question until I had longer to consider it, I bluffed, "I'm not really concerned about that, just now."

"You will be," said Graham, repeating it for maximum impact, "You will be."

Observations

- A corporate strategy for exploiting IT is focused on value, money and people. IT gives it a scope but it is not about technology.
- The directors of a company are an interdependent community of value creators.
- Value is a portfolio of types and measures.
- The money that an organization spends on IT is, in business terms, a random number.

SIX

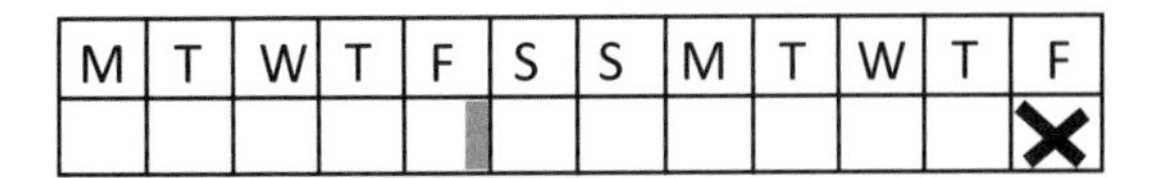

Still wobbling a bit from Graham's between-the-eyes prediction, even though I already knew it to be true, I called Barry again to tell him about the numbers Graham wanted. I also mentioned that Graham had remembered him for always saying 'nonsense'. It's funny what people most notice about someone else that forms the basis of their perception and relationship. I wondered what people most remembered about me and how much people like Juliette and Graham knew - and used - the impact they had on others.

"Hmm," said Barry, "so we need a table of projects with a column for type of business value and another for total business investment? And we're allowed to leave the business investment blank?"

"Only if we don't know what it is. Isn't that in the business case?"

"Hah! Very funny. There's a figure in the business case that we use to calculate the Net Present Value, to keep our friends in Finance happy."

"Let's use that then."

"I'm not sure it's accurate and we never revise it afterwards. We're always re-estimating the IT investment."

"OK. Let's have two columns for total business investment – one for the business case number and the other for the latest estimate. Leave the second one blank."

"Sounds a bit dodgy. Won't that leave us exposed?"

"Possibly, but those aren't our numbers."

"And this P&L thing?"

"I think he means the impact each project will have on our IT service costs and on IT depreciation."

"Service cost is another one where we stick it in the business case but don't take much notice afterwards."

"Well, put in the business case figure, unless the project manager knows any different."

"Will do. I hate to think where all of this taking us. You know it probably means working all weekend."

"Yes, thank you."

I left our offices and walked round the corner to my favorite coffee shop. Armed with a decaf white Americano and a conspiracy theory, I sat down in an armchair to ponder the answer to Graham's question about my role. Maybe I was being set up.

Scenario one: This was all a game after all, to secure my exit from the company.

Scenario two: I was being used as a catalyst for something else and would eventually be in the same role as I already had.

Scenario three: Juliette and Graham really wanted me to take on a new role.

Scenario four: Something else I hadn't thought of.

I tried to call Helen on her mobile phone and then her landline at work, but all I got was her voicemails. What would she have said if I had been able to talk to her? Stop being so self-centered and paranoid, I expect. Start by taking the situation at face value, then run through the scenarios to see if they changed anything.

Christine and I had established that my role (if it continued to exist) was to be one of the 'we' in Graham's Promise, together with the other executives on the demand side of IT. A customer, not a supplier or even someone the customers spent their IT money on. So I and they all had to be involved in creating and maximizing value and in IT spending decisions. No we didn't. I remembered Graham's concerns about the multiple WEs in the Promise. The people maximizing value wouldn't necessarily be the same as the ones spending the money. Perhaps the WE/NOT WE technique had served its purpose, if only to emphasize that the right split to be thinking about was between customers and suppliers, not 'the business' and 'IT'. And that I was to be one of the customers, managing their strategy for exploiting IT, whatever that strategy promised. Juliette had said that 'enabling' value did not promise enough and Graham had told me to stop acting like a supplier, even though I had people working for me in supplier-type roles that we could outsource if we wanted to. But the reason I'd used the word 'enabling' is because people in IT are not in a position to create any real value. That was always going to be someone else's job - in Marketing, Sales, Finance and so on. All we IT people could do was provide them with the tools to do it. Except that providing tools for other people to use is exactly what suppliers do, isn't it?

I was stuck, clearly missing something that I felt certain Juliette and Graham had already worked out. I needed to think some more about the meetings I'd had with them. Graham had said that they wanted to use the problems we had with IT to solve a wider business issue about creating value from investing in change, and that would solve the IT problem anyway. Their strategy: IT as a Trojan Horse, but inverted. The inside, friendly strategy visible, the outside (presumable less friendly) hidden.

IT = Inverted Trojan (Horse). Interesting Tactics.

That seemed to summarize it nicely, but beyond this neat analogy my mind was still blank.....

.

.

.

.

.

.

Nothing.

I went over to the counter to buy another Americano, and a chocolate croissant. The girl who took my order was wearing a Happy to Serve You badge with her name, Kimberley, on it. She was tall, with freckles and long wavy blond hair tied back in a pony tail. Like the other staff, she did indeed look happy to serve me, which was why I liked to come here. I was reminded of Graham's service versus services explanation.

"You look deep in thought."

"Yep, Kimberley. Sure am."

"I always write things down when things get heavy. Otherwise I can never work it out."

"Me, too."

I paid her for the coffee and went back to my armchair. Kimberley was right, I ought to write down some more thoughts or draw some more pictures, something other than just sit and think blank thoughts.

About twenty-five minutes later, I had filled up a page with a muddle of thoughts and questions, and with a red pen circled these:

Accountability for creating value (from IT)?

Investment different from spending?

Who makes (IT) spending decisions?

Customer of IT

- Getting good service from IT
- Investing in change/IT
- Spending with IT suppliers
- Minimizing/optimizing cost
- Creating value from IT
- Customer's strategy: maximize return on investment.

Supplier of IT

- Delivering IT products & services
- Creating IT
- Receiving money, maybe subcontracting to others
- Being efficient (unit cost of supplying something)
- Supplier's strategy: keep customers spending; make money.

I seemed to be getting somewhere. Frankly, though, I'd had enough, so I never did get back to my scenarios and went home for the weekend instead.

Observations

- Many perceptions and relationships are based on a few high-profile characteristics.
- Customers of IT expect service; service level agreements with IT suppliers are necessarily about services. Using the coffee shop analogy, where's the service element of IT?
- Corporate and business strategies are ultimately about numbers. Make the strategy for IT the same.
- In many companies, the people creating value are not the same as the people spending the money. Which is your strategy primarily about?

SEVEN

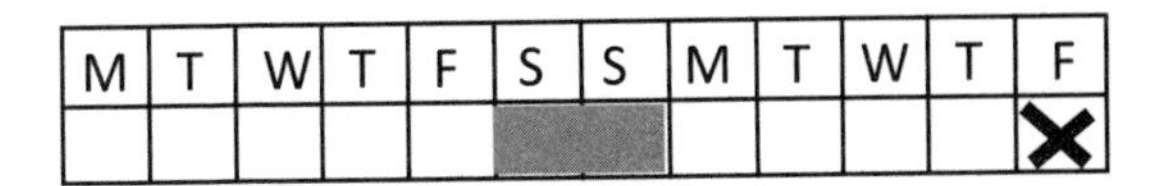

M	T	W	T	F	S	S	M	T	W	T	F
											X

On Saturday and Sunday, I looked at my notes a few times, but I didn't seem to get any further. I still couldn't see what my new role was supposed to be, nor did I figure out which of my coffee shop scenarios was most likely to be true.

I called Barry twice over the weekend. He was making progress and unexpectedly enjoying himself. I asked him why. It was because there were some things he'd wanted to say for a long time, some deep frustrations with the way projects were conceived and managed. The idea of using the numbers to show people what we did and didn't know had given him a relatively safe way of expressing what he had been feeling in a way that executives would easily understand. If he wasn't Operational-Environmental before, he was showing signs of it now.

I had a round of golf on Saturday and was rubbish, and a game of tennis doubles on Sunday and sparkled. My tennis partner was aglow – she also played much better than usual – and our opponents were left wondering what had hit them. I mention this because I'm quite a good golfer and a terrible tennis player.

Perhaps all this talk of turning things on their heads was getting to me.

Observations

- Numbers offer a dispassionate way of illustrating the strategic landscape, what we know and don't know, and what may need to change.

- A process of change at work is likely to impact the non-work lives of the people involved.

EIGHT

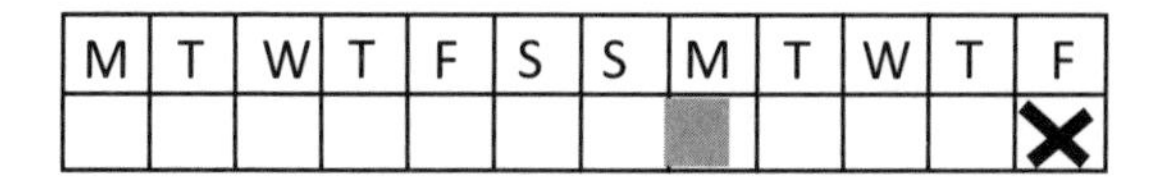

At about half past eight on Monday morning, Christine and I met on our strategy sofa again, coffees and croissants in hand. Outside the window the sun was striking the Thames through broken cloud cover.

"How was your weekend?" she asked.

"Good, thanks. Yours?"

"Likewise."

"So we're seeing Graham at four this afternoon. He wants us to say why we think the company is not already achieving his Promise and what, in principle, needs to be done about it. I spent some time after we finished on Friday thinking through everything, including the question about my role in the WE community. I made some progress, but don't have the answer yet. I've never produced a strategy that fundamentally questioned my own purpose in life, especially one that's an inverted Trojan Horse."

It was a really clumsy link but I wanted to tell her about my Trojan Horse brainwave.

"Pardon?"

"IT. Inverted Trojan - as in Horse. Interesting Tactics! Inside strategy visible, outside strategy hidden. I came up with that on Friday. What do you reckon?"

"Clever, but I'd let it drop if I were you."

"Why?"

"It seems to devalue what Juliette and Graham have asked you to do. From what you've told me, I not even sure that it's an accurate picture of the strategy they have in mind. Did they tell you that they were going to keep their wider intentions a secret?"

"No, they didn't."

Christine was beginning to look like a much better strategist than my Strategy Manager. Simon would have loved the Inverted Trojan (Horse) idea. I showed her the notes I had made in the coffee shop and we spent over three hours talking them through as well as the muddled thought processes behind them. I told her I thought the WE/NOT WE technique had taught us what we needed to know, and she was happy to leave it there. Then we turned to the other notes we had made together on Friday and started to make connections. We also talked briefly about the strategy's impact on my role and, by implication, on her own. Strangely, perhaps because of Graham's very direct challenge on Friday or my ponderings in Kimberley's coffee shop, I was now finding the subject of my future role much easier to handle.

Lunchtime arrived and I told Christine that I wanted to formalize our discussion as preparation for our meeting with Graham, so we split up for a couple of hours.

I bought a tuna sandwich and an orange juice from the staff restaurant, took it downstairs to the visiting directors' office on the ninth floor and plugged in my laptop on one of the two desks. Frank, our Director of Procurement, was at the other desk. He asked me what I was working on and when I said "strategy" he just replied "Ouch".

Here is what I wrote, taking a whole hour despite much being recycled from the notes Christine and I had written on Friday:

Promise: We will maximize the value we create from all the money we spend on IT.

Who are we? The directors of the company, including me. But is every We in the Promise the same group of people?

Why is this Promise a challenge?

- We don't understand the connection between spending money on IT and creating real value for customers and shareholders.
- IT is treated as a discrete investment/spending 'stream', yet on its own delivers no value.
- Business cases for 'IT projects' are used to get approval for money that people want to spend on technology.
- Nobody is truly accountable for, or rewarded for, delivering the value of a project.
- Our IT team has a built-in conflict of interests, trying to be both customer and supplier at the same time.
- There is nobody looking after the investment 'big picture'.

What do we need to do?

- Map the connection between spending money on IT and creating business value: i.e. expose the business plan driving the IT plan.

- Merge IT spending (investment?) into everything else (???).
- Rethink the way we use business cases.
- Reward project managers differently – anybody else?
- Separate the IT team into two.
- Get somebody managing the big picture.

Bearing in mind the final bullet, I also decided to work on my identity crisis.

Who am I?

- One of the 'we', the customers of IT
- Maximizing value, making investments or spending money?
- Chief Information Officer? Doesn't sound like it…
- Chief XYZ Officer? What's XYZ?

I phoned Barry to find out how he was doing. He was just finalizing the figures to send over to me.

"What do they tell us?"

"Depends what you want to know. At the moment, the Total Business Investment column looks a bit lightweight. It's just over 50% more than the total IT investment, and I'm sure we must need to invest much more than that to get all the benefits of our projects."

"What do you think is going wrong?"

"The first thought that struck me was that, except for in IT, we don't ever track the actual time that people spend on projects rather than day-to-day operations. So we've got nothing concrete to go on to estimate how much of their time it takes to get the project from idea to deployment, and then to deliver the benefits. We've got only one department - us - capturing our employees' time on projects. I always thought that was best practice, but if so, why is nobody else in the company doing it?"

"Interesting thought. Don't our IT Business Analysts make the estimates?"

"Yes, and I've had a chat with one or two this morning without saying why. They reckon it's because everyone sees IT as the main investment, so they are always likely to underestimate the non-IT costs. And anyway, they'd be less likely to get their business cases approved if they made better estimates."

That triggered me to wonder about the financial principle of Prudence – to estimate all probable costs and only those benefits that are certain. After all, it was James and his finance department that were the main designers and enforcers of the project appraisal process. However, I kept these thoughts to myself and chose a different angle.

"I suppose that the ratio between IT and non-IT costs is unique to each project."

I was beginning to agree with Graham's random number theory about IT.

"Yes. In some cases the total business investment to deliver the benefits must be many times the IT figure and is bound to need re-estimating as the project progresses."

"Do you have an example?"

"Well, APEX1, actually. I know I moaned to you about it on Friday because the scope keeps changing. I reckon the costs of getting enough value out of it for the project to be worthwhile exceed the IT investment by a factor of at least four or five. Yet nobody is recalculating any of this as they keep on changing their minds about what they want it to do."

"Tactics. Changing their tactics."

"No, changing their minds. I agree it would be changing their tactics if they did a proper evaluation of the consequences, but they're not. They expect us to do it for our bit, and give us a hard time if the IT costs go up or the delivery date changes, but that's all. From the point of view of Return on Investment I've no idea whether APEX1 is still worth doing or not, and politically, I'm not in the best position to ask."

"Now that's an interesting insight. Going back to the timesheets, do you think we should get everyone doing them?"

"Yes and no. It would help us be more certain about the total business investment in projects, and track the consequences of people changing their minds, or tactics, but it's time-consuming and difficult to achieve. Remember how awkward it was just to get IT to do it? We even had to fire some people before everyone took us seriously."

"Yes. Food for thought."

I thanked him for his weekend's work and told him to email the figures to Graham and me, which he promised to do right away.

I called Christine and we met up on the sofa again. We used the time remaining to talk through the notes I had produced, which she seemed very happy with. Stupidly, I forget to tell her about my conversations with Barry and even the one with Lawrence. Then we went to see Graham.

Observations

- Strategy is not everyone's idea of fun.
- Formulate the strategy through re-iteration and evolution.
- Look for the numbers to speak for themselves.
- Explore how your company budgets for, manages and measures business change projects involving IT.

NINE

M	T	W	T	F	S	S	M	T	W	T	F
							▌				✕

Graham wasn't there. His PA, Judith, told us to sit down and brought us some coffee. At twenty-past four, Graham arrived and started talking while he took off his jacket, caught his breath, smiled and sat down.

"I'm sorry I'm late. You must be Christine. I'm Graham. Great to meet you. Ian, how's it going? What have you got for me?"

I handed him a copy of my one-page summary. He sat back in his chair and put one foot up against the edge of his desk, leaned an arm on his knee and read it.

"This is good, Ian. Let's talk about it. Firstly, I think you need to go for the jugular a bit more."

"For instance?"

"OK. I think your tactics are fine as far as they go, but I reckon they are pussy-footing around the heart of the problem. Christine, unless you only came here to listen, what do you think?"

Christine looked over at me and I gestured for her to speak out.

"What I see when I work with the business is that nobody's really taking accountability for delivering the benefits in business cases."

"Who do you mean by 'the business'?"

Déjà vu.

"The operating units, corporate business functions, you."

"Doesn't that also include you? You made it sound like it doesn't."

I cut in. "IT departments in general refer to everyone else in the company as 'the business'. Christine and I know that we are part of 'the business' really."

"You'd better stop referring to everyone else as the business then."

"I'm sorry," said Christine.

"Good. Now let's get back to what you said about accountability and business cases. In that respect, you're absolutely right. That's one part of the problem we want to solve and we think you, Ian, are best placed to solve it."

"Getting people to take accountability for delivering the value promised in business cases for IT projects?"

"Close, but no banana. Firstly, you've been telling us for ages that there is no such thing as an IT project. How does it go? There are no IT projects, just business projects with IT components. Secondly, the problem isn't limited to projects involving IT, it's true of all our internal investments."

"What you mean by internal investments?"

"Yes, Christine, good question. I mean all the investments we make to sustain and improve the performance of the company, not those where we invest externally in, say, another company. You're looking worried, Ian."

"Sorry, I frown when I'm thinking things through. It sounds like you want me to take on the job of making people accountable for delivering whatever value they have promised in their business cases, whether or not their project involves IT."

"Holding, not making, people accountable - that's part of it, but don't focus too much on your own role just for the moment. Let's rewind for a minute and I'll tell you what Juliette, James and I have in mind."

"James is in on this too? Actually, why isn't this his job, as CFO? Oh, by the way, I've booked a meeting to see him tomorrow afternoon."

Graham suddenly looked at me differently than before. I noticed I was beginning to blurt things out and needed to slow down.

He replied to both my questions at once. “Because although this is something that needs to be done separately from Finance, you obviously need to be in close collaboration with him. Anyway, here’s what we want to do. The end game is to make sure that we maximize the value of all our internal investments, not just on a project-by-project basis but across the whole lot. We want to start with those projects that include IT because everyone sees a problem with them, in particular…”

I thought about protesting and it must have shown.

“I know, it’s not fair. IT isn’t the only thing we have a problem with. We have the same issue with all sorts of business change projects. But IT is an easy target and one that everyone sees as a problem, so we’re going to hit it first. And with that as the first port of call, we already have you in place to take the lead. That’s if you want to, of course.”

When had I said that I didn’t?

“I’ve been wrestling with the question of my role, so I’m not sure what leading this strategy looks like yet.”

"No problem, old boy. In your shoes I'd be feeling quite vulnerable, but I did want you to think it through before today."

"That's OK. Let's see if I get the picture now. You want me to manage a strategy where the ultimate promise is to maximize the value of all our internal investments, starting with our projects involving IT."

"Lead, not manage, but otherwise spot on. A couple of things to add, though. The strategy will be a success when maximizing the value of our investments is firmly embedded in our investment culture and day-to-day running of the business. We don't want to achieve the Promise, celebrate and then regress. Also, it will be interesting to see how much of a challenge is left when we've solved the problem for projects involving IT. Ideally, we should have learned all we need to know if we get the IT side of things sorted, making it a relatively painless process to widen the scope to everything else. That is, in essence, our strategy. Are you up for it?"

This whole conversation was moving very quickly. I asked Graham if I could have a few minutes to get my thoughts together.

"Sure. Christine, let's grab a coffee. Do you want one Ian?"

I asked him for a decaf white without. They left the room together and I decided to go for a walk to the restaurant to look at the view, rather than stay put.

"Hey, Ian. Didn't know you were here today. How's it going?"

It was Simon, my Strategy Manager, being overtly jovial and a little unnatural.

"Yes, good, thanks. I'm just in a meeting with Graham"

"Did you see that Titac Systems have released version 12 into beta testing?"

"Yes, I did."

"I think we should offer to help them evaluate it. I've been dying to see what's different. It could change our whole strategy."

"OK, give me a call later and let's talk about what's in it for us?"

"What sort of time?"

"Not sure, but before six-thirty. If you don't catch me then, give me a ring on the mobile first thing tomorrow."

"Will do. Fancy a coffee?"

"No thanks, Graham's just getting one for me. Speak to you later."

Simon walked off to get a coffee at the bar, and I looked back out of the window. What a contrast. Sorting out the company's fundamental problems with internal investments versus beta testing Titac 12. Both in the name of strategy. No wonder Juliette and Graham had asked me what kind of strategist Simon was.

I thought I'd better go back to Graham's office, as I hadn't told him I was disappearing for a walk in the first place. Because of the conversation with Simon, I'd missed the chance to think through what Graham had asked me. Maybe I should have told Simon I didn't have time to talk.

As I walked back along the corridor that led to Graham's office, I wondered why I hadn't let on to Simon that Christine was also in the meeting with Graham and me. I suppose I didn't want to upset him again, especially as he had seemed to be trying hard to look happy. Back in Graham's office, there was still nobody there. I sat down and waited. A few minutes later Graham and Christine came back, Graham politely standing to one side to let Christine walk through the door first.

"How are you doing, Ian? While you were thinking we've been having a chat. Anyway, you first."

"I went for a walk and got collared by Simon talking about beta testing Titac Systems' new software release. It highlighted the enormous difference between the kind of strategy we've just been talking about in here and the sorts of things that we sometimes call strategy in IT."

"I'm sure there's value in both of them, and there's bound to be a connection somewhere along the way."

"Can we go back to your question? I haven't had much chance to think it through, but I think the answer is yes."

"Good. I was hoping you would say that. Christine and I were talking about how all this affects the work she's been doing. I think there's a real chance that we'll be able to make good use of some things that you and she have been working on."

"Yes, Ian," said Christine "that work we started on investment planning is probably going to be the backbone of making this new strategy succeed. Graham wants to see it as soon as possible. Is that OK?"

"Sure. Of course. No problem. Now what I think I want to do, when we've finished this meeting, is to sit down with you again and put together a rough draft of the strategy we discussed before you both went off to get coffees, as best I understand it. I need to get my head around the practical implications."

I turned back to Graham.

"Can I come back to see you again later?"

"No, I'm sorry. The next chance we have to meet is Wednesday morning at ten. If you're going to start developing a draft strategy, I'd like to tell you how I would prefer to see it structured. Do you mind?"

"Go on."

"Basically, I want to see three things. Promise, Principles and Tactics. The Promise is the one you already have, unless you can think of a better one. Mind you, I think you should resolve the potential confusion of the multiple WEs. And it must be a promise, not a statement of intent or aspiration. The next step is to say what strategic Principles - or truths - we all need to follow. With the Promise and Principles, we'll have the stable core of our strategy. Then we can finally add the more fluid part - the Tactics you think we need to execute to get us there. At this stage, we just want tactical themes, not chapter and verse. Obviously, from the thinking you showed me earlier, you already have some of those. Oh, and remember to be clear about your rationale. You know, the key strategic issues - and opportunities - as you see them and why we should choose the route you're recommending to deal with them. You don't necessarily have to write all of that down, just the Promise, Principles and Tactics, but be ready to talk about your rationale if anyone asks."

"You just said to use the Promise that you gave me last Friday, which is all about IT. What about the final end game, when we roll the strategy out to all our internal investments? Doesn't that change the Promise, or do we intend to keep it under our hats?"

"No, we will tell everyone what we intend to do in the end. We don't want to play games or keep it a secret. Why would we do that? But I want you to stick to the Promise about IT. I tell you what, in your introduction make it clear what the ultimate goal is and say why we are starting with IT. In effect, there might be a second stage in our strategy to follow this one, but there's no need to worry about it yet. Remember, we don't know how much of the total problem will be left over when we have sorted out the investments involving IT."

"I'm seeing Marianne and James tomorrow. How do you want me to handle them?"

"Are you seeing them together or separately?"

"Separately."

"Not sure why I asked really, those two avoid each other as much as possible. It's a finance and marketing thing. But if you were planning to see them together, I would have told you to see them separately. It works better at this stage to talk things through with each person individually. Why are you seeing them?"

"Marianne called me when she heard from Juliette that I was revamping the IT strategy. I booked the meeting with James after we had our discussion on Friday."

"Don't feel that you need to hide anything. Juliette and I have discussed all this with James anyway, so I'll leave you to decide what you want from the meeting with him. Now what about the figures from Barry?"

"He finished a first-pass over the weekend. They should be in your Inbox by now. I was having a chat with him a few minutes before we started this meeting."

"What do they say?"

"He's still looking at them, and he's struggling to know what we want them for. He did notice something, though. He thinks that our projects are underestimating the total business investment needed to deliver their benefits. For example, we in IT are the only people keeping reliable records of the time we spend on projects rather than day-to-day operations. It seems odd that only one department is doing this and nobody else. Our IT Business Analysts reckon there's much more time being invested outside of IT than we're accounting for in business cases. Also, as people change their minds about the projects they're doing, they're not recalculating all the potential consequences. It's possible that some projects are becoming unviable in terms of return on investment, but we don't know, so we're not doing anything about it."

"You've got business analysts? So have I and so has James. I wonder what yours do that's so different. Don't answer that one now. Let me see if I can bring up Barry's numbers."

Christine and I waited quietly while he plugged in and opened his laptop. I caught her eye at one moment, and she tried to give me a discreet but meaningful frown. Graham glanced at her. I'm sure he noticed something, but he didn't react.

"Right, let's see. Oh. Damn. He's got this the wrong way round."

"Why. What's wrong?"

"He's got the IT projects as the rows and the types of business value as a column. It needs to be the other way around. I suppose that's the IT-centric mindset for you. I must remember to be more explicit next time. Make the IT into columns, not rows."

"Why does it need to be the other way around?"

"Because we need to start by thinking about our value portfolio, then the business investment projects for achieving it, and finally the IT elements of those projects - if there are any. No wonder we've got such problems with our investment culture." He continued without checking whether I had understood what he'd said. "Ask him to swing the whole thing round, and do some totals by type of value. See what that tells us."

Christine gave me a gentle kick under the table. I had no idea what she was trying to tell me.

"OK," I said.

"Good. Well, that's all I've got time for today."

"Thanks, Graham. See you on Wednesday."

"I look forward to seeing your next draft and whatever else we've managed to get from the numbers. Good luck, old boy." He turned to Christine. "See you soon, dear."

"'Bye, Graham" said Christine, with a cheery smile and a glow in her eyes.

Observations

- The basic strategy framework used here is Promise, Principles and Tactics.
- The Promise and Principles are the strategy's stable core; its Tactics are more fluid in light of events.
- In the initial formulation of a strategy, engage each key stakeholder individually before then engaging them as a group.
- Lead the execution of a strategy, don't manage it.
- Two planning principles for investments in change: Start with value and work backwards; make IT into columns, not rows.

TEN

M	T	W	T	F	S	S	M	T	W	T	F
											X

As Christine and I left Graham's office she took me by the elbow, dragged me into a nearby meeting room and half-slammed the door.

"When were you going to tell me about the work that you've got Barry doing?"

"What's the problem?"

"If you'd told me what was going on we could have avoided Barry getting it wrong. We had already sorted out the basic template in the investment planning work that I led before. So on the one hand, I'm telling Graham about that and on the other you've got Barry doing what amounts to the same thing but making basic errors for all the world to see."

"Graham is not the whole world." As I said this she started to react, so I held up my hand to stop her, "But you're right. Graham asked me to get the project numbers from Barry late last Friday and he's been working on them all weekend. I didn't add two and two together, didn't realize the connection with the investment planning work."

"And you're the one always reminding us to get our communications ducks in a row before talking to people outside of IT. That's been a fundamental part of my job."

I had to accept that she was right. I had always been ruthless with people in IT who went around the business giving contradictory messages, undermining our credibility. This was one of the main reasons that I'd established the Business Partnerships team, to make sure we presented people in the business with a united front. Now here I was doing the opposite with one of Juliette's inner circle. It was time to mend the damage and up my game.

"Now that I think about it, I've also asked Lawrence to compile some numbers that Juliette wanted. It's time to get the three of you working on this together."

As I told her what I had asked Lawrence to do, it was obvious that this was also closely related to the work Christine had done before. With hindsight, I should have paid much more attention to the connections.

She was calmer. "I'll have a chat with Barry and Lawrence and make sure we're working to one set of figures. I'm not saying that this is the same as the work we did before – there are some angles we didn't explore or even think about. But the basic frameworks are likely to be the same."

"Yes, please do that. Meanwhile I'll carry on with the overall strategy."

She suggested that we wait until I had seen Marianne and James before trying to write a draft of the strategy. She didn't think it would take that long – she reckoned that if it ran to more than three pages we were probably on the wrong track. I thought of the seventy-eight pages that I had given Juliette and it suddenly occurred to me to ask how many pages the company's overall Corporate Strategy covered. Christine left the meeting room and I went back to Graham's office. Luckily he was still there, although he had said he wouldn't be.

"None."

"What do you mean, none?"

"You sound surprised, in fact I'd say almost angry. What makes you think we would write down and publish our overall Corporate Strategy?"

"How else will everyone know what it is?"

"The people that need to know, do. The rest, I'm afraid, is too much of a risk."

"But you must write something down."

"Actually, yes we do, but it's never the entire strategy. From a competitive and commercial risk perspective, that would be stupid. Anyway, the only person who will ever really know the entire strategy is Juliette. That's her job."

"To know the strategy?"

"No, to be the strategy."

Graham was beginning to lose me again. How could someone *be* the strategy?

"So where can I look?"

"Firstly, in our Report and Accounts. Both Juliette and the chairman summarize the key points of our strategy each year so that our stakeholders can see what it is. Also, I can let you see, in confidence, the latest Board presentation updating the non-executives on our progress. Finally, if you look at everything that Juliette writes and says you'll see that she's always reminding people what our strategy is all about, if they happen to be listening. So although we have no one document officially covering the end-to-end strategy, much of it appears in many places. Apart from the risk issue, we also think that's much better than having a strategy document that people read and put on the shelf. We need to make sure we are all applying the strategy to every decision we make and in everything we do.

Otherwise we don't have a strategy, just a document saying what we intended it to be."

"I always thought the document was the strategy."

"People do."

"Christine and I were thinking of writing a short paper for Juliette and you – perhaps about three pages. Is that still a good idea, then?"

"Yes, it is – but only so we can have something tangible to talk about when we meet with Juliette and James on Friday. The shorter and punchier the better. It doesn't have to answer all the questions we might ask. In fact, it should provoke us to ask the right kinds of questions, instead. Sometimes we learn more from the questions we ask than the answers we get. So write it with the three of us in mind and be prepared to talk us through the practicalities of anything you think we need to be doing differently to make the strategy work. A key thing to think about is how best to make the strategy come to life for everyone else – issuing them a strategy document may help a bit, but it's never going to be the full answer and may even do more harm than good if we're not careful. We have to make it personal."

"Why?"

"Because people will quickly forget the strategy, or even be cynical about both it and us, unless we make it have a real impact on their day-to-day working lives. A document on its own is not going to do that. It's too passive. So before very long, the strategy will have no credibility because it never actually happened. In fact, we want the strategy to light some fires, cause some new battles – battles which it then has to win."

Graham was starting to show that glimmer of excitement again. To me, it was all starting to sound a bit dangerous.

Standing up to leave, I said "OK – thanks. That's given me enough to go on until Wednesday."

"See you then."

As I turned to leave Graham's office, I caught sight of him smiling to himself.

Observations

- If you are the strategist, then you are the embodiment of the strategy.
- Foster collaboration around one master set of strategic themes and numbers. Eliminate duplication and fragmentation.
- Make the strategy personal to each individual who can influence its execution. A document is unlikely to do this.

ELEVEN

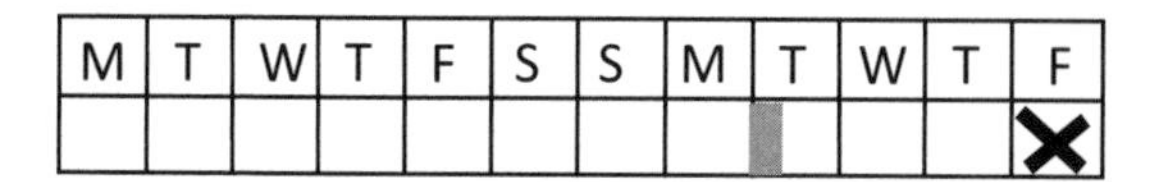

M	T	W	T	F	S	S	M	T	W	T	F
								▮			✕

I don't think it's ever a good idea to have sex with someone you work with, and I'm pleased and relieved to say that I never have. But Marianne and I came close once, we really did. Not, as is so often rumored to happen, at an overnight corporate event in a hotel. No, we just fell for each other when we first met and started a personal relationship, before deciding that it was not a wise way for two executives at the same company to behave. I know other people do it, but that's for them to decide. We went as far as planning a holiday to Mauritius together and then cancelled it.

I'm telling you these private details because they were still relevant to our working relationship four years later. We had both been new to the company at the time and neither of us was married back then. Helen and I had not even met. Without any commitments at the time to other partners, Marianne and I could have legitimately gone the whole way, even gotten married. But since we remained work colleagues, I think both of us are glad that we didn't.

With this in mind, I found it ironic, although I don't mean to be unkind, when Sharon - our IT

Business Partner for Marketing – used to tell us all that she owned the IT relationship with Marianne and Marketing. No, she didn't own my relationship with Marianne and I doubt that her relationship with Marianne will ever be quite as personal as mine once was.

Out of courtesy, though, I phoned Sharon first thing on Tuesday morning and told her I was seeing Marianne for lunch.

"What's the meeting about, Ian?"

"Strategy. Marianne wants to tell me something about strategy, but I don't know what. Any ideas?"

You can tell I was deflecting questions from Sharon by asking them myself.

"No, she hasn't mentioned it to me at all. Maybe it's about the new marketing database. That's of real strategic importance to her. Would you like me to call her and ask?"

"No, that's OK. I can do that myself if I need to."

"I'd like to sit in on the meeting, if that's OK."

"It's a lunchtime chat, Sharon, not a meeting as such, so don't worry."

"OK." She didn't sound OK.

Somewhere along the way, the IT Business Partner thing had gone awry. I never meant people like Sharon to 'own the IT relationship' with the directors and business units that we assigned them to. They were just supposed to make it easier for people to work with us in IT. If they didn't know who in IT to speak to, or were struggling to get what they wanted, they could ask their IT Business Partner for help. If they did know who to speak to, there was no point. We all work for the same company, after all. And nobody can 'own' a relationship other than the two people whose relationship it is. As for having a relationship with 'IT', well we had over three hundred people in my IT department, not counting people on temporary contracts and outside suppliers, so I wasn't sure what that really meant. If we were still going to have IT Business Partners in our new strategy, then Christine and I would have to rethink what they did.

While Christine, Barry and Lawrence were off compiling the numbers, I thought I had better revisit Christine's previous work on investment planning. She had run a pilot project in one of our business units with a Finance Director called Harry, and one of our IT Business Analysts. They had used some innovative ways of presenting the numbers, which had stimulated new thoughts in the business unit's executive team. I needed to remind myself where they had gotten to and why we stopped. Back at the hot desks, I plugged in my laptop and after a bit of searching found the files on the Network.

She and Harry had already answered one of Graham's questions, at least from a local business perspective rather than the corporate one. They had compiled a list of nine types of value and started to find out what milestones the business unit had for them in its business strategy and operating plans. They had called the list of value types and milestones their 'value portfolio', although by the time the work stopped they had not discovered many milestones.

They had also dealt with the 'make IT into columns not rows' principle that Graham mentioned in a simple but effective way. In their original spreadsheet, just like Barry's, the rows were IT projects. They weren't even business projects that included an IT element. Most of them had IT-sounding names like 'Core systems refresh' and 'GTS 3.1 Upgrade', and showed only the IT costs (but, interestingly, the Net Present Value of the business project as a whole).

They gave a 'dummy' business name to each project (Project A, Project B, etc.) as most had names that would make no sense to a non IT-literate executive or manager. Then they swung the basic spreadsheet around by 90 degrees and made it into a simple matrix with the value portfolio as the rows and the projects as the columns. Finally, using the information in each project's business case they had shown which primary type of value the project was promising to deliver and any secondary contribution. Summarized on a presentation slide, it looked like this:

Value Creation Matrix - Projects Involving IT

Type of Value	Projects Involving IT													
	A	B	C	D	E	F	G	H	I	J	K	L	M	N
Revenue protection & growth	●			○	○						○	○		
Cost control & reduction	○				○		○		○			●	○	
Productivity & Efficiency		○				●	●		●				○	●
Brand reputation		●		○						○				
Customer delight				●									○	
Employee delight					●		○							
Compliance - legal & regulatory			●						○	●			○	
Survival							○			○	●		○	
Business Infrastructure	○				○			●		○		○	●	

● Primary motive for project

○ Secondary contribution of project

Source: Project business case

Looking at this matrix again, some observations immediately came to mind:

- Out of the five projects that were contributing to revenue protection and growth, only one had this as its primary motive. What if the others, with different primary motives, failed to make their contributions? Also, from the perspective of our revenue milestones, were these five projects being managed as a coordinated portfolio to make sure they made the best collective contribution and didn't double-count benefits?

- Project M seemed to be trying to do almost everything all at once. How could it be contributing so many different types of value, and at the right time in terms of our business plans and value milestones? What did its benefits realization plan look like? Perhaps it was really only an Infrastructure project and it would have been better to say so.

- The Productivity and Efficiency row was unique by having more than one project with that type of value as its primary motive. How did we conceive of these four particular projects and were we putting all these eggs in the right basket? (No, as it turned out when Christine and Harry presented their findings to the business unit executives. I'll tell you about that in a moment.)

Then they had done a four-year IT investment total for each type of value in the portfolio, for the current year and the next three and expressed it as a percentage of the grand total. They called this summary the business unit's "De Facto IT Investment Strategy". If you're more familiar with working in US dollars, multiply these numbers by two.

De Facto "IT Investment Strategy"

Type of Value	New IT Investment	% of Total
Revenue protection & growth	3.4	11.0%
Cost control & reduction	1.0	3.2%
Productivity & Efficiency	13.3	43.1%
Brand reputation	0.6	1.9%
Customer delight	2.5	8.1%
Employee delight	0.4	1.3%
Compliance - legal & regulatory	4.7	15.2%
Survival	1.3	4.2%
Business Infrastructure	3.7	12.0%
Investments are in £million	30.9	

Although the numbers they were using were just the IT investment in each project, not the total business investment, there did seem to be some logic to what they had done. The question they had posed to the business unit executives was 'does this seem like the right kind of profile for our new investments in IT, given the types of value we want to create from them?' I'd been at the meeting where they had presented their conclusions and had asked this question. When presented with their de facto 'IT Investment Strategy', the executives' collective view was that it didn't look right. The investment profile did not seem to reflect their priorities for using IT to create value, nor their beliefs about the business unit's on-the-ground abilities to exploit IT in this way. One of them also asked a question we had not considered. Given that we were looking three years into the future, how come there was no provision for investment projects we would expect to be doing, but we didn't know yet what value we would need them to add. An 'unassigned' value type, if you like. We noted the question but never did anything with it because the process went no further, for reasons I'll explain.

Martin, who was that business unit's Managing Director at the time, said he was stunned by the 43% of new IT investment that was going into improving business productivity and efficiency. When Christine asked him why, he replied that there were two reasons. Firstly, he didn't think he needed to make any new investment in IT or anything else to hit his productivity and efficiency milestones. He could hit those milestones with existing operations, using investments that the business unit had already made. Secondly, he didn't have any evidence to show that people in his business unit really knew how to use IT to improve productivity and efficiency. In fact, there were signals to the contrary. Investing in IT seemed to dent the business unit's productivity ratio rather than enhance it.

Martin proposed cancelling the projects that were promising to improve productivity and efficiency. The IT money that they represented was to be diverted to other projects delivering different types of value or kept in the bank. At that point the process died - I think because some of the people there, and many others, had invested a lot of themselves in the projects that Martin was proposing to cancel and because the IT investment plan was not significant enough in itself, to make everyone, including Martin, feel that it was worth the grief.

With the benefit of the conversations I'd now had with Juliette and Graham, I thought we had been following the right principles and process but with the wrong numbers. Even if we had still limited ourselves to those business projects that involved IT investment, had we used the total business investment numbers I think we would have had a better chance of engaging the business unit executives in not just the theoretical exploration of their de facto investment strategy, but in the execution of their conclusions. I also thought that Martin should have toned-down his response when the de facto investment strategy looked the wrong shape. Perhaps a better tactic would have been to debate which projects, if any, to cancel and let all the other ones continue to their intended conclusion. At least we could have then used the existing projects as cases in point, to explore and conclude the right principles and process for new projects, and then improve things progressively rather than killing the process stone dead.

Embarrassingly, when I thought about it in hindsight, I had internally cheered when Martin had said we should cancel a load of projects that were investing in the wrong kind of value. At last, I had thought, someone else could see what we had been trying to tell people all along.

As I reviewed those document and events, Martin's tactical error - assuming that's what it was - now seemed very obvious. Or maybe I had misread his strategy and he achieved the outcome he wanted (to preserve the status quo). And he was now the Managing Director of our largest business.

It was time to have lunch with Marianne.

Observations

- A relationship is 'owned' by the two people involved.
- Using innovative ways of presenting numbers can expose previously hidden knowledge.
- Establish the primary value contribution of each project and any secondary contributions.
- Build a bottom up value portfolio.
- Expose the 'de facto' investment strategy to drive discussion of strategic priorities for exploiting investments.
- Prepare ahead for the consequences if the 'de facto' investment strategy looks wrong to its stakeholders.

TWELVE

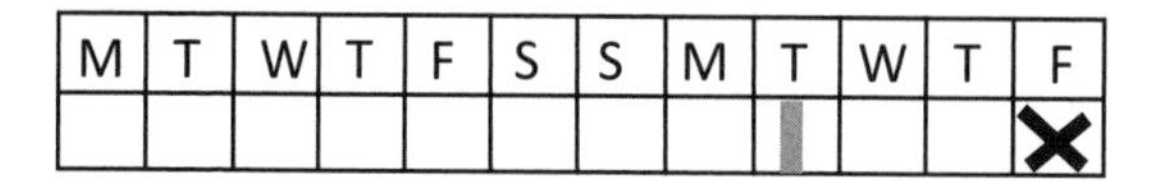

M	T	W	T	F	S	S	M	T	W	T	F
											X

Marianne is about five feet three inches tall with curly dark hair and blue eyes. She always wears a skirt and heels and people think she is trying to look taller. She isn't, she just likes the shape of her legs better when she sees them in heels. The people that think she is trying to look taller badly misjudge their dealings with her. She's a strong lady and people would do better if they spent time getting to know her rather than rush to judgment based on their own preconceptions.

We each decided on a salad for lunch - hers tuna, mine chicken - and made small talk as we queued up to pay. We found a round table near a window and I sat facing the world outside with Marianne taking the chair on my right, not opposite. She is left handed and I'm right handed, and we know which way around to sit to avoid clashing forks and elbows.

"So, I hear that our illustrious leader is getting you to rethink the IT strategy." On a personal level, there was no love lost between Marianne and Juliette, yet professionally, they worked together very well.

I decided to wait for Marianne to say something else.

"Aha. It's the 'you'll have to ask me a direct question' look." She paused for a couple of seconds, smiling, then said, "OK, what has Juliette asked you to do?"

Remembering Graham's advice to be straight if asked, I told Marianne the essence of the story so far, as we munched our salads.

"That's a tall order, Ian. Where are you going to start?"

"I don't really know yet. At the moment I just have few notes and a team working on the numbers. But by Friday, I have to see Juliette again with Graham and James and she'll want to know the complete answer."

"No, she won't. I expect she'll first want to make sure that you're all still talking about the same basic problem, that you have an overall strategy for dealing with it and that you, Ian, are going to work as an equal with the rest of us to make it happen. Let's face it, you've been hanging off to one side of the executive team since I've known you. On the one hand, you've wanted us to treat you as an equal and on the other you've been behaving like a bolt-on. Juliette and

Graham will want to see that you're now prepared to join in and get your hands dirty like we all have to."

"I do get my hands dirty. I run almost all of the company's IT systems, manage a staff of three hundred, plus loads of suppliers and have a budget of over £100 million a year."

"Yes, but that's our money, not yours, and we could get someone else to do most of the things you people do if we wanted. You know, outsource it and concentrate on core competencies."

"Like marketing, I suppose."

She smiled. "Absolutely! But let's say we did outsource the entire IT department, you included, we would still be stuck trying to use IT to create value with nobody of our own left to guide us."

The picture Marianne was describing reminded me of the two circles that Christine and I had drawn in response to Graham's draft Promise.

"So do you think we have given ourselves a problem by having IT as one department trying to be on both sides of the IT demand/supply equation?"

"IT demand/supply. I hadn't thought of it like that, but yes I can immediately see what you mean. You seem to be mainly stuck in some kind of internal supply mode and we need to you to be one of us on what you call the 'IT demand' side. But that's an awful name for it."

"Why is it awful? What would you call it?"

"There's something negative about the picture it conjures up. It sounds constraining rather than inspiring. In terms of communication and messaging, it's just a no-no. We need to think about how to articulate your strategy in a way that inspires people, not makes them go flat or negative. I'm sure we do have to constrain our collective demand for investment and that's useful when it comes to deciding our priorities, but I'm not sure why it should only apply to IT. How about simply calling it investment management?"

"Does it really matter?"

"Yes, of course it does." I must have looked pained, because she put her knife down, put her left hand gently on my right wrist for a few seconds and then took it away again. "Sorry, I didn't mean to sound patronizing. We'll have to choose our strategic language carefully and think about what certain words mean – like 'demand management' – to the people listening. And it's not just the words. They also infer a different picture. Regulating demand for investment is a key consideration in investment management, but demand management doesn't encompass value creation in the way that investment management does. I'm a very visual thinker and in the way I picture things, demand management seems to be primarily concerned with what goes into the funnel, whereas investment management is primarily concerned about the value we create at the other end. And if we're determined to maximize the value we create from our investments, we'll be regulating demand automatically.

All I'm really trying to say, with this example, is that language and communication are going to be really important in executing the strategy Juliette has asked you to formulate. If I know her way of doing things, she will expect you to start next week. She doesn't muck about. "

"Juliette doesn't muck about. Is that strategic language?"

"Absolutely!" She laughed.

I paused while we ate some more, then continued, "I'll think about all that demand management stuff. Thanks. Anyway – you were talking about the meeting I have with Juliette, Graham and James on Friday. You don't think they'll want to know all the answers?"

"James is already involved? Good luck. I think Juliette will want us all to explore what the strategy means as the first part of its execution. She will expect you to have come up with something we can use to do this exploring so we can guide you on where to go next."

"Any ideas?"

"Nope. Sorry. Just make it practical, not theoretical or abstract."

"I suppose what's practical, theoretical or abstract depends on the audience."

"That's right."

As time for lunch was quickly running out it occurred to me that Marianne had originally texted me to discuss something and I still did not know what it was.

"What was it you wanted to talk to me about? You know, when you sent me the text last Thursday?"

"That was it. Juliette and Graham wanted me to have a chat with you about language and communications. When your strategy hits the fan, there will be a lot riding on how you put it across to the rest of us."

I remembered my phone conversation with Sharon. "Don't you want to talk about the new marketing database?"

"No, thanks. Let's stick to things of real strategic importance."

"I thought it was. And you keep telling Sharon that it is."

"In a narrow marketing sense, Sharon's right, it is. But if we don't get your new strategy right, it will probably be a waste of investment just like everything else."

I thought about mentioning that she had sponsored the project and signed off on the business case, but thought better of it.

"I know I'm the project sponsor and would never say publicly what I just told you. It's the right project to be doing, but I'm pretty sure that we won't make the most of it. I'd probably be ostracized by the culture if we did. We're all suffering from this same issue and we know it. Juliette was right when she told me it had nothing to do with IT, really. I can't wait for you to sort it out once and for all. I just can't wait."

Observations

- Each stakeholder in a strategy has something distinctive to offer.
- Language and communications are critical to a strategy's success.
- What's practical, theoretical or abstract depends on the audience. Adjust the way you articulate the strategy according to who's listening.
- People in companies are often doing good projects but are not making the most of what those projects deliver. It may be counter-cultural to do so.

THIRTEEN

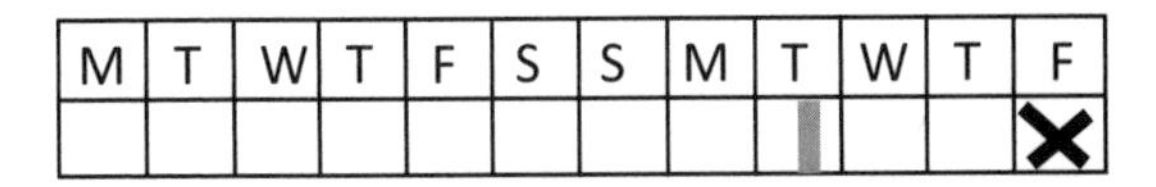

With the Marianne lunch under my belt, the next stage in the journey was my meeting with James.

Marianne didn't like James, but I did. I know that CIOs and CFOs are meant to be sworn enemies – at least if you read the IT press – but he and I got along well. We are about the same age and have some common interests, both professionally and personally. People think that James is very serious-minded because in public he's generally quiet and doesn't often smile. They're partly right, but I was there when he started cracking puns and firing off-the-cuff humor, and then he was probably one of the funniest people I have ever met. His favorite line is when someone asks him how he is, he says 'never better', and when they say 'good' he replies 'I never said it was good'. Gets them every time. Ha, ha. It must be the way he says it.

The previous CIO and James definitely hadn't gotten along at all. When times had been harder and everyone else was trying desperately to make the company more efficient, the CIO seemed to be finding ways to justify and grow the IT budget at every twist and turn. All he did was to make himself everyone's enemy. People suspected that he had much more empathy with the IT supply industry than with the other directors of the company he worked for. By comparison, my own 'supply-side' sins seemed fairly harmless. I very much doubt that Juliette would have asked him to lead the 'internal investments' strategy. I think he would have been one of the first to undermine it if he thought it might direct money or control away from IT.

Just before heading to James's office, I rang Simon. Suddenly remembering one of the many things Juliette had challenged me on in our meeting, I wanted to ask him what the impact would be if we assembled our IT roadmap from the business units' investment plans.

"That's not right. You know they haven't got a clue what they are going to need in the future. It's a recipe for disaster."

"But if they don't know what they need, surely we can't either. That would seem to be an essential principle for our roadmap. We can only know as much about the business priorities and plans as everybody else."

"What about the maintenance we have to do that's not driven by the business unit investment plans? It sounds like you're suggesting that we should stop planning for that. Then where would we be? It is, after all, about 80% of our IT investment plan."

"That's a fair point. But presumably we're doing it on their behalf, to mitigate risks to their businesses. If we explained that to them, I expect they would either integrate those projects into their investment plans or we might have to think again. Anyway, it's only 80% of our total investment by chance, not choice. Now I think about it, it strikes me as an odd choice to try and make. For example, we could make the 80% into 67% just by doubling the investment in creating new value. Or by reducing the total investment pot by 40%, while continuing to invest 20% of the original total in creating new value and finding cheaper ways to mitigate the same risks as before. We'd do better to explore and target these two basic categories of investment separately from each other, rather than put them into a dubious ratio. But your basic point still stands." That was funny: I hadn't ever thought of it like this until prompted by Simon's challenge.

Simon didn't want to pursue the numbers line any further. "This conversation is worrying me, Ian. I think we are in grave danger of giving up the control over the IT agenda that we spent years building. I'm not keen on this laissez-faire approach you are considering. If I may say so, I think you're beginning to go native with the business."

These were strong words coming from Simon. And he was speaking them with a shaky edge to his voice.

"Thank you for your thoughts, Simon. But I think we have to make very sure our investment plans are driven by our own business strategies not those of our IT suppliers. I've made no decisions yet and I'll bear in mind everything you've said."

The conversation ended there and I walked down the corridor to James's office.

"Hello James, how are you?"

"Never better." However, he wasn't smiling and I didn't care to bite anyway.

"Me, too."

He continued with unusual formality.

"I am going to come along to your meeting with Graham tomorrow. We want Christine to tell us about the work she was doing on investment planning. Where did she get to?"

"News travels fast. It started when she was doing the three-year plan with Harry. But after a promising start it died a death and she's struggled to make an impact with it anywhere else."

"Why didn't she come and tell me about it. I would have given her an honest view on its value and helped her develop it further if it seemed a good idea."

I was reluctant to tell James that Christine was nervous about coming to see him, simply because he was the CFO and she wasn't sure whether she and Harry had gone out on a limb. I think she had had a nasty experience with a previous CFO who had castigated her for getting involved in things that he saw as the province of Finance, not IT.

In the end, though, I decided to be straight with him. "I think she has been concerned that she and Harry had gone out on a limb, and that you would give her a hard time. She doesn't know you as well as I do and I think she had a problem with a CFO in her previous company. Didn't Harry mention anything to you?"

"No, he didn't, but that's a bit typical. He's very good at what he does, but like a couple of the other FDs, he tends to try and keep me and my team out of the loop when it comes to the internal affairs of his business unit."

"Won't that give us a problem when we get going with the strategy that you, Juliette and Graham want me to lead?"

"Yes, it will. You'll need to help us work out how the strategy is going to deal with that particular problem. How have you managed to make it work in IT?"

"I'm not sure we have, really. Our IT Business Partners have made some progress, but because they work for me, people are not sure what side of the fence they actually sit on, so don't always tell them the whole story. In some ways, having them has reinforced the gap that we intended them to bridge. I suppose it says something that people think there is a gap between us and them in the first place."

"You're mixing your metaphors, but I know what you mean. I think the fence, or gap, will always be there, but because you are a corporate function like us and not because you are IT. What did Harry and Christine come up with?"

"When you see her tomorrow, I'll make sure she's prepared to tell you better than I can today. She and my team are also resurrecting it as we speak, to help compile some numbers that Juliette and Graham wanted. We originally started it because we were trying to work out the value of IT and Harry's business unit was interested in doing the same. We'd looked at some industry models, but they all seemed a bit conceptual. Even if they came up with an answer, we weren't sure what we would be able to do with it."

"How can you put a value on IT?"

"That, James, is the interesting question. It's fairly easy to value technology assets for the balance sheet and measure the performance of IT services. But that's not the same as calculating what technology is worth to us as a business in terms of the value we create from it. There are quite a few people out there who think that you must be able to do this, looking for the magic formula to tell us all the answer. Maybe they're right, but I don't think so."

"Why not?"

"You can tell I'm a bit cynical. I think it contradicts a really simple principle, which is that IT, on its own, delivers no value. If you believe in that principle, then trying to put anything other than a book value on IT just looks to me like an illogical thing to attempt, and a complete distraction from looking at the right question, which is the value of what we do with IT – not of IT itself. That nobody has given us a really compelling answer yet should tell us something. Also, many of the people working on the question seemed to have a vested interest in there being an answer which makes IT valuable."

"Such as?"

"IT suppliers and technology consultants, for a start." James nodded. "So we decided to try something else. Rather than start with IT and put a value on it, we wanted to start with value and see where IT fitted in."

I told him the rest of the story, glad that I had revisited the papers earlier.

"So you think it stopped because Martin reacted like Attila the Hun, taking his axe to the projects people had set their hearts on."

"Yes. Everyone said what a great exercise it had been and then they left it there."

"That's a pity. It sounds like a good way of addressing the IT-value question. Why didn't you suggest to the meeting that they take a less drastic and more considered approach? "

"At the time, I mentally agreed with Martin's answer, not realizing it would kill the process. My people and I get really frustrated with people wasting the company's IT investment on projects that are either the wrong ones or that they're never going to make the most of." I moved to change the subject. "Although that initiative didn't work out, the experience does now give us a significant advantage in planning our new strategy, one that we wouldn't otherwise have. It will help us see why our strategy will be difficult – and what battles it will have to stir up and win."

"I am not sure that the IT department is best placed to decide which investment projects are right or wrong. In any case, by Friday I think you must complete the numbers that Graham has asked for."

"We're trying our best to do just that."

"It will make the whole thing more tangible, less fluffy. In the end, numbers is what makes Juliette and the rest of us tick."

"I'll let the team know that you're supporting what they are doing and re-emphasize the importance of coming to a conclusion by Friday."

"Good," said James and just looked at me.

It seemed that we had finished, so I broke the silence by chatting with James briefly about family and holidays, and called it a day. It only occurred to me afterwards that he had not once mentioned explicitly whether he thought the new strategy was a good idea, or whether I was the right person for the job.

Observations

- Strategy is about options and opportunities. It's not usually about being 'right'.
- Take the lessons from what didn't work as expected.
- Someone's relationships and interactions are affected by previous events and experiences.
- Look for the subtleties in people's responses.

FOURTEEN

M	T	W	T	F	S	S	M	T	W	T	F
											X

After the sessions with Marianne and James, I phoned Christine and told her what James had said about the numbers. She said they were getting on fine and would have something to tell me by the next morning.

There was one other person I wanted to talk to, if I could, before meeting up with Graham again on Wednesday and then preparing for Juliette on Friday.

I might be 'hopeless' at strategy, to quote Juliette, but Justin isn't. He's an old colleague of mine who had retired three years earlier, although he was only fifty, and then went around the world as a strategy trouble-shooter, helping executives to see why their strategies weren't working as well as they would like and to rethink their tactics.

I phoned his mobile number and was lucky. He was in Spain, only one hour ahead. He answered after the fourth ring.

"Hello, Ian. I'm in a restaurant in Barcelona, so apologies for the background noise."

"I'm sorry to interrupt, but I was hoping to talk something through with you for a few minutes. Can I call you back later?"

"No, let's do this now. It must be important or you wouldn't be calling. Hold on while I step outside."

"Thanks, Justin."

I waited while he walked through the restaurant and out into the street, hearing a background melange of foreign voices and the clattering of cutlery on china.

"That's better," he said "I can hear you now – can you hear me?"

"Yes, I can, thanks."

"I'm in a little back street, so it's fairly quiet – not much traffic. How well do you know Barcelona?"

"Not at all. Never been to Spain."

"Don't let them hear you say that. This may be technically part of Spain, but it's really Catalonia. Proud people. I do like it here. I'm in the gothic quarter. Very old with lots of narrow winding streets. A brooding sense of ancient pleasures and dangers. But anyway, what can I do for you?"

"Some advice, please."

I spent a good ten minutes talking him through the chain of events, starting with the Juliette meeting the previous Thursday ("I bet that seems like a long time ago, eh?", he said – and it did), all the way up to the meeting with James and my afterthought about his support, or apparent lack of it.

"OK," he said, "I've got all of that. What's the question?"

"Am I being set up, Justin? What do you think?"

"Maybe, but it doesn't really sound like it from everything you just told me."

"What could James's problem be?"

"Who says he has a problem? But I'll go along with your paranoia for now. If he has, it's probably one of two things. I think he might be wondering whether the role that Juliette is asking you to perform really comes under his domain and whether this new strategy is some kind of indictment of his performance. After all, making sure the company is managing its finances to get the best return is really what a CFO is there to do, isn't it? That's the first possibility. The second is that he is so used to IT people trying to formulate and execute their strategies at arms length from everyone else rather than by collaborating, he might be worried that you are going to do the same with this one. What do you think?"

"The first one sounds more likely. He has been imposing controls in our project approval process based on delivering a minimum Net Present Value - NPV - and everyone has been applying them in business cases. But what he hasn't done, now that I think about it, is taken a great deal of interest in how valid people's NPV calculations really are and whether people actually deliver the real-life benefits their project promised. So I suppose he's been letting people off the hook."

"That's a bit harsh. Putting people on a hook is not going to be the best way to motivate them. Let's assume that people are conceiving of good projects, but are not focused enough on shaping and executing them to create the maximum value possible. I expect what James hasn't done, by the sound of it, is embed a desire to deliver a maximum return on investment into the company's management culture. Just putting a control like NPV into business cases won't do that. All it's likely to do is to feed the current culture. Are people using NPV to justify projects they want to do anyway, or as a tool for helping to assess the best value projects to invest in when everything else is equal?"

"The former. Justification."

"It seems to me that a key plank of your new strategy is to challenge the justification culture. James may be either an asset or a liability, depending on how he feels about the new strategy in terms of his own role and performance and the way you are going about it. So also bear in mind your second potential reason for his apparent reaction so far. Make sure you do the opposite of what he may be expecting. Collaborate."

"OK."

"Back to the NPV thing for a moment. When you were talking to James, did you test with him your observation that value is a portfolio of measures?"

"Yes. Well, sort of. Actually no, not really. Graham already gave me a steer on that one. It was wrapped up in my summary to James of the investment planning work we started with one of our business units."

"That died a death."

A statement, not a question.

"Yes, if you want to be that brutal about it."

"Tell me if I'm wrong. So you didn't ask him about the relationships between your value portfolio and NPV, and he didn't say?"

"That's right. In fact, I didn't even make the connection between the investment planning story and his policy on NPV."

"Sounds like you need to sharpen up, Ian. Your strategy is already in play, impacting people's feelings and behaviors and you don't even seem to know it."

He was right. I was being tactically naïve and missing Graham's 'little moments'.

"Thanks, Justin, that's all I need. Oh, no, one last thing. What have all these financials got to do with a strategy for IT? Both Juliette and James mentioned them."

"From the sound of where this is all taking you, everything. You need to choose a number that your strategy is all about and that you're prepared to take accountability for. It won't be the IT department budget any more. When all this is over, there probably won't be one. Nobody, including Juliette, Graham and James, may know what that number actually is, yet – either in terms of its scope or scale. So you decide what you're going to pitch for. It may all hinge on that."

"That's it. Thanks again. Please go back to your meal. I've taken up enough of your time."

"Not so fast. I've one last question I'd like you to consider. Why you?"

"Because I'm the CIO and they want the first stage of the strategy to be about IT."

"That might be part of the reason." He paused, and I waited quietly. "Let me see if I can answer my own question. I think it is also because you have a rare – maybe even unique – perspective over all the changes that take place across the organization. You currently only see the ones that involve IT, but it does mean that you have a big picture view that nobody else has. It may also be personal – because it's you."

"But Juliette keeps telling me I'm hopeless at strategy."

"Yet it sounds like they have you on a crash course to change that."

"Could be. Thanks for the vote of confidence."

"No problem. I'm going to leave you now. Give me a call in a month or so to tell me how it's going."

"Where will you be?"

"I have no idea. Beyond next week, my calendar is empty."

"Doesn't that bother you?"

"No, because it always seems to fill up as much as I need it to."

"What if it doesn't one day?"

"Plan B. And if that fails, Plan C."

"What are Plans B & C?"

"Now that would be telling. Bye."

"OK, Justin", I smiled, "goodnight."

Observations

- Expect a corporate strategy to be, in part, about culture change.
- As you formulate a strategy, you're already executing it.
- Explore potentially different reasons for people's responses.
- Always have plans B and C for keeping your strategic Promise.
- The CIO role has a unique perspective on business changes around the company.

FIFTEEN

M	T	W	T	F	S	S	M	T	W	T	F
											✕

I woke up on Wednesday morning in a bit of a sweat.

Only two days to go until the next meeting with Juliette and I only seemed to have a vague shape in my mind for the strategy she had asked me to prepare and on which my future career in the company depended. The conversation with Justin had highlighted how important the nuances of relationships, company politics and financials were going to be. Graham had indeed said, right at the outset, that it would be all about money and all about people.

Also, I hadn't arranged a pre-meeting with Christine before we met with Graham and James, or even briefed her on my lunch with Marianne, only my meeting with James. Sometimes I think I am just hopeless.

As soon as it seemed reasonable to do so, I gave her a call - about 7:45, as I walked along the street heading for the office. Before I could tell her anything, she asked me how the meeting with Marianne had gone and whether we were going to meet up before seeing Graham. Magic.

"Marianne told me something interesting that I'd rather share with you in person. Oh, and James is joining us for the meeting with Graham."

"Good. Can you and I get together as soon as we're both in the office? I'm almost there now – where are you?"

"I'm nearly there as well, let's meet up in the restaurant."

As we sat down, Christine produced two copies of some spreadsheets and summary charts from her bag. She, Barry and Lawrence had concluded the most relevant ways they could think of for me to present the numbers on Friday. She commented that Barry, who knew of the work that she and Harry had done before, was concerned that Juliette might also be tempted to shelve lots of projects. While I didn't know what Juliette would do, I felt she would be more understanding of the consequences than Martin had – superficially, at least - appeared to be. I told Christine that I understood Barry's worries, but that we would just have to wait and see. I would be lobbying for us to take a more measured approach this time, if the same situation occurred.

"It was difficult to know how far to go in showing the total business numbers, rather than just the IT ones. We decided that, for the projects portfolio, we would partly take Graham's original advice and show what we know about the total business investment but not to have a second, blank column. Instead, we've included a footnote hinting at our concerns. We've also chosen not to use the current names of projects, as they are mostly IT-centric. We've just allocated them letters."

"Like you and Harry did before."

"That's right. We want to focus people on what the numbers tell us. We can easily explain the dummy project names and how we'll make them meaningful later. Have a look – see what you think." She handed me the first summary sheet. (As I mentioned before, if you'd like to get a feel for the scale of these numbers in US dollars, double them.)

Internal Investments Portfolio - Extract

Scope: Projects involving IT costs

Type of Value	Projects	Value	Total Investment (see note*)	IT Cost Elements: Project	IT Cost Elements: Service Costs Impact
Revenue protection and growth	Project A	£13.5m	9.2	8.8	+0.21
	Project B	£131.8m	15.6	9.2	+0.37
	Project C	£17.8m	8.1	3.3	+0.03
Cost control and reduction	Project D	£26.7m	2.4	1.8	+0.19
	Project E	£183.7m	13.5	9.2	+1.44
Productivity & Efficiency	Project F	+0.31	8.9	6.8	-0.35
	Project G	+0.63	7.4	6.0	+0.16
	Project H	+0.15	3.4	1.7	+0.18
Brand reputation	Project I	+3.0%	4.5	0.0	+0.63
	Project J	+8.0%	4.1	2.7	0.00
Customer delight	Project K	+0.21	5.5	2.9	+0.86
	Project L	+0.16	5.0	3.3	+0.23
Employee delight	Project M	+10.0%	4.8	0.2	0.00
Compliance	Project N	Yes	4.2	2.4	+0.42
Survival	Project O	Yes	0.3	0.1	+0.19
Infrastructure	Project P	None	18.0	14.9	-0.77
Investment figures are in £m			114.9	73.3	+3.79

*From project business cases: except for the IT element, not subseqently re-estimated.

Christine summarized what the sheet was showing me. "We've settled on these nine types of value, based on the benefits that projects are promising in their business cases. As it says, these are only the projects that involve IT costs, so there may be other types of value that we haven't found yet. Also, we don't know whether a top-down approach would come up with the same ones."

"Graham said he would think about it from that angle."

"Each type of value has a different overall measure of performance. Some are financial, some are percentage-based ratios and others indexes. There are a couple which are yes/no evaluations and one - Infrastructure - where there's no obvious value measure at all. For each project we've shown the value it is promising to deliver, the total business investment proposed in the business case and the IT element of that investment. These investment numbers comprise both capitalized and expensed project costs. We've also shown how much each project is expected to increase, or decrease, annual IT service costs."

After I had taken in what the sheet contained, I commented, "I like the way you color-coded the overall business plan differently from its IT implications. Also that the business investment includes the IT element. Let's make sure we do both those things all the time. The total business investment - even if it's not accurate - is obviously the number we should be using to prioritize the portfolio, not the IT total. Graham said he thought the IT total was a random number. I wanted to disagree with him at the time, but now I can see why he was right. Damn! Why didn't we come to this conclusion ourselves, ages ago?"

"Don't know. What else do you see?"

"As you said, the measure of a project's success is obviously different depending on the primary type of value it is promising to deliver. We've been using Net Present Value to choose which projects to invest in and that doesn't seem to be right. What if our strategies depend on projects that have low NPVs? I bet some of the projects on this list are NPV-negative, if we're honest. Like compliance projects or infrastructure. Even Brand, unless we have a proven formula to link percentage increases in Brand reputation with cash flow. On another subject, the IT service cost impact is interesting for a couple of reasons. Firstly, we're not explicitly holding our projects, in total, to an agreed total impact on service costs. Secondly, we're not checking and agreeing with business units on how they want to share this additional cost so that they can account for it in their forward business plans – or indeed challenge it before the projects are delivered and it's too late. You know, there's a lot to explore in this one sheet."

"And in the other one, too."

"What's that?"

"Lawrence has put together the best numbers he can for the total costs of IT to the company's P&L and cash – not just the portion that comes through the IT department's budget. This represents the true scope of whatever corporate strategy for IT we might want to have. Strategically, the IT department budget is a red herring, as it's about 68% of the total that we've found so far. I'm sure we ought to apply a strategy to 100% of the company's IT costs or perhaps not bother at all. And with the way IT is going, I think more and more costs will be tucked away in business units, rather than channeled through the corporate department."

"Why?"

"Because we're still acting as if we can control the technology that people use and what they use it for. Yet for years and years, since we introduced client-server technologies in the late 1980s, decision-making and power has been shifting away from IT departments into business units and then out to external customers. If we say no to something the people in our businesses really want to do, because of our strategy or budget, they will get it done anyway. They may even call the investment something other than IT to avoid problems."

"OK, so what do the numbers say?"

"Based on current plans, the three-year impacts of projects on IT costs to P&L and cash are significant – even after we've offset them with operational efficiencies on the spending side. A big increase on both counts."

"How big?"

"In three years' time, the costs of IT to P&L will be about 52% higher than today. The costs of IT to cash will be 35% higher."

"Why is one percentage higher than the other?"

"They're made up of different numbers. The P&L cost includes depreciation but not capital, whereas the cost to cash is the opposite. Let me show you the numbers." She handed me a second sheet:

IT Costs to Profit & Loss, and Cash

£ million	IT Costs: This Year Capital	This Year Expenses	Year +1 Capital	Year +1 Expenses	Year +2 Capital	Year +2 Expenses	Year +3 Capital	Year +3 Expenses
Projects	53.8	19.5	62.1	21.2	58.9	22.7	71.4	28.5
Services*								
Service costs		*32.4*		*36.8*		*38.9*		*42.6*
Deprecation		*26.9*		*38.7*		*42.1*		*48.3*
Sub total - Services		59.3		75.5		81.0		90.9
Total Cost to P&L		**78.8**		**96.7**		**103.7**		**119.4**
Cost to Cash	105.7		120.1		120.5		142.5	

**Including the incremental cost impacts of: business change projects, business volume changes, spending efficiences and supplier price inflation*

Christine summarized this sheet for me. "So here we have just the IT costs to P&L and cash. There's no broader business context, but this provides a simple overview of where the total IT costs come from and how the figures inter-relate. All the main moving parts, if you like. The key point is that if we want to constrain or influence the totals at the bottom, we need to understand the causes-and-effects behind them. For example, depreciation is caused by capital investment in projects. So we can constrain that element of the P&L total by investing less capital in IT. But that has a business implication that this sheet doesn't show. So if we use it correctly, this way of representing the IT costs shows, on the one hand, the inter-dependencies between those costs, which is useful, but also helps to demonstrate why considering IT costs in isolation is a flawed process. These costs are rooted in the business decisions that cause them."

I looked at this sheet for a minute or so before commenting. "You've used the same color coding as the other sheet. Good. That helps to highlight all these numbers as just the IT implications of the business investment plan, not the entire plan. Now, for the numbers themselves. It immediately strikes me that if we don't like the three-year outturns for costs to P&L and cash, we'd better start working on them now."

"That's right. These costs are a medium- to long-term consequence of business events and decisions. There's a limit to how much we can change Year +3 by the time we're into Year +2."

"Why isn't the increase in service costs on your Portfolio sheet the same as any of the differences here? I can't make the two join up."

"As this sheet says, the movement in service costs is caused by a number of things, not just the projects Portfolio. The figures that are the same are those for projects. The total new IT investment on the other sheet is the sum of the current year's capital and expenses for Projects on this one."

"Ok, I've got that now. But then shouldn't we break the service costs down to show where the movements are coming from"?

"We can, but I think that's getting into too much detail at this stage. Please can we go back up a few levels and understand where all this helps with the new strategy?"

I had to admit to Christine that I still wasn't sure. Perhaps if I could take away the work that she, Barry and Lawrence had done, then I could figure out the connection. As a last resort, I would have to ask Graham why he had told us to do the numbers this way.

Then I found myself thinking of Justin's advice about choosing a number to be accountable for and Juliette's original questions about the IT budget, and an intuition suddenly emerged.

"You know, we were doing the WE/NOT WE thing with the Promise the other day. When it talks about maximizing the value we create from all the money we spend on IT, which number is that?"

"The value or the spend?"

"The spend."

"Let me think."

Christine looked again at her spreadsheets, and thought for a while before answering, “I think spending means how much we actually pay to suppliers and employees, so that would be what we’ve called the cost to cash. Is that the right number for our strategy to be founded on?”

“I don’t think so, but I’m not sure why. Anyway, it’s the same basic number as our current IT budget, only bigger because we’ve included all the company’s spending on IT, not just the part that’s channeled through the IT department’s budget. Let’s say we change the Promise from ‘spend on IT’ to ‘invest in IT’. What would that do?”

“It would mean choosing a different number to found the strategy on, although I don’t know which one or even whether it would be right.”

“Neither do I, so let’s leave it for now. I’ll do some more thinking about that later.”

I put my copy of the spreadsheets and the two summary pages into my briefcase and wondered whether there was anything else that Christine and I should talk about before our meeting with Graham. Without thinking especially hard about how she might react to it, I decided to tell her about my lunch with Marianne.

When I told her what Marianne had said about the marketing database project, Christine's eyes hardened and she stared out of the window for a few moments. When she didn't say anything for a whole minute, I asked her what she was thinking about.

"Sharon's been working night and day on that project thinking that Marianne was committed to its success."

"I know….."

"So what did you say to her, then? Did you challenge her on our behalf?"

"No, I didn't….."

"Well on behalf of Sharon and me, thanks for nothing!!"

"Before you chew my head off any further, can I please explain why I think Marianne and the other directors are doing this?"

"Doing what – lying to us about how important things are and making us work our socks off for things they don't believe in?"

"The company investment culture is what's at fault. Graham's mentioned it. Marianne is just fitting in with how things work. At least she is prepared to admit it to me, albeit in private, and should support us sorting it out. At the moment, I think that anyone who did deliver a maximum return on an investment in IT, or anything else, would be seen as too clever for their own good and out of alignment with everyone else. Not delivering a return on investment and blaming it on IT is currently one of the things people have to do to fit in. And we, in IT, have been playing along with it too. Riding to the rescue when we should have been clear about our accountabilities and stuck to them. So we've ended up as scapegoats."

Christine just sat and looked at me for a while. All I could do was wait and see what happened next. After a long couple of minutes, she stood up with a blank red face and tightly announced:

"I'm going to the ladies room. Back in a minute."

"Do you want coffee?"

"No. Yes."

She walked towards the nearest door and, as an afterthought, called out "Please" over her shoulder, without looking back.

While Christine left to sit and reflect, I walked over to the counter and bought two coffees. Outside, the sun was still quite low, lighting up the undersides of the clouds that decorated the sky here and there. There was a television over in the other corner of the lounge with the volume muted. A silent weatherman was pointing enthusiastically to thunderstorms in the London area.

I went back to the sofa where we had been talking and sat down. Christine came back and remained standing. Looking down on me, she said:

"I'm thinking of resigning. Tell me why I shouldn't."

"Please, sit down."

"No, thank you. I'm more comfortable standing up."

"I don't want you to resign. I think you are the best chance we have of making the new strategy work. And I think it is what you came here to do – but maybe not in the way that you expected."

Silence. She just at looked at me with shiny red eyes - I don't think she even blinked.

"Christine, please don't resign."

More silence. Then she turned and walked slowly over to the floor-to-ceiling windows and put both hands on the glass, fingers apart, arms straight, looking out. I left her there for a while, then walked over to stand next to her. I leaned my left shoulder on the window so I was facing her sideways-on. With the windows slanting outwards, it felt like I was about to fall to my death.

I said gently, "We are due to meet Graham and James in a quarter of an hour. Even if you think you are going to resign, please could you come to the meeting with me and tell them what you have been doing. They want to know. If you decide not to stay and see it through, we will need to find someone else who can. I'm not sure how easy that will be."

She turned to face me with her eyes still hard and slightly narrowed, her lips pushed together, and slowly nodded once. Without any trace of humor in her face, she said quietly, "You must trust that glass a lot," then turned around, walked slowly over to the sofa and sat down again. "What do you want me to do?"

"Just talk Graham and James through the work you did with Harry before and what you learned as a result. Then show them the spreadsheets we looked at earlier. See what they ask."

"Right. And can I talk to them about the Marianne thing?"

"Let me deal with that."

Observations

- Use color coding to distinguish the overall business investment from its IT elements and implications.
- Show why the IT investment total is the wrong number to use for prioritization decisions.
- Highlight that strategically important projects may have low or negative financial returns on investment.
- Proactively manage the overall impact of the portfolio on future costs to P&L.
- Expose why managing the costs of IT in isolation is a flawed process.
- Show that the costs of IT to P&L are a longer-term consequence of business decisions, and need proactive forward management.
- Explore the causes-and-effects linking IT numbers with overall business investments and the creation of value.

SIXTEEN

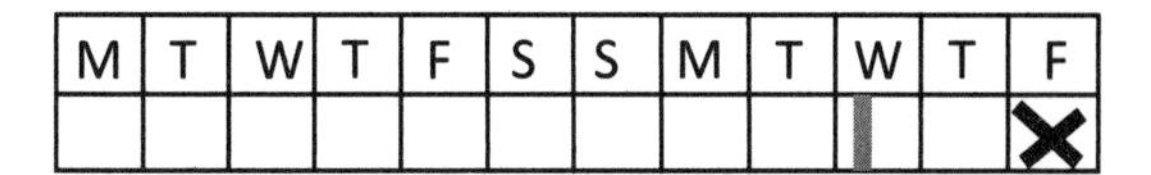

I thought the meeting with Graham and James was strange, but seemed to be successful, as far as it went.

Graham appeared much less interested in the strategy compared to earlier meetings and James sat through the two hours we all spent together saying almost nothing.

We started with Graham asking me how things were going. Mainly for James's benefit, I summarized the work that Graham had already heard about in our meetings on Monday. I then talked about my lunch with Marianne and the importance of language, without yet mentioning the comments that had so inflamed Christine to the point of wondering whether to resign. Finally, I said that James and I had met the previous afternoon and that we were both agreed on the need for the strategy and the basic way forward – looking at James to cut in with his own version of events, but he just nodded without saying a word.

Christine talked to them about the investment plans that she had worked on with Harry and they both asked a couple of questions about the mechanics of compiling them and what value anyone had derived from them. She admitted to them that the process had come to a halt after the first presentation to the directors in Harry's business unit and nothing further had happened. Then she showed them the new work she had done with Barry and Lawrence. James asked her to meet up with him the next day to talk about it some more. I suddenly felt my ownership of Christine's work beginning to slip away, but I had too much left to do before Friday to join in with the meeting that James was suggesting, and anyway he hadn't invited me. I would have had to invite myself and I thought that would appear defensive.

When she had finished, Christine turned her head halfway in my direction and gave me a meaningful, expectant look. Was I going to raise the Marianne question?

Which I did, and offered the same perspective as I had given to Christine earlier, on what this meant about the company's investment culture. Graham and James caught each other's eye and Graham told me he was sure there was probably some merit in pursuing this question with Juliette and perhaps to raise the subject again in the session with her on Friday.

The meeting finished at midday, on schedule, with no great flourish or significant agreement. I asked Graham if he fancied some lunch, which he did, and the two of us went off to the staff restaurant together leaving James to go back to his office and Christine to head off again for Windsor.

Observations

- Who's accountable for the energy behind a strategy?
- Qui pro quo: be prepared to give up something to get something else.

SEVENTEEN

M	T	W	T	F	S	S	M	T	W	T	F
											X

"What happened? Where did all the energy go?"

As we sat down at a table with a sandwich and a drink each, I was desperate to know why the atmosphere had apparently changed.

Graham looked at me without any obvious expression for a few moments, and then said, "Now that's funny, Ian, I was going to ask you exactly the same question."

"But on Monday you seemed interested and fired up for this, and yesterday even James seemed five times more engaged in the subject than today."

"Well, so far Juliette, Marianne, James and I have all given you permission to get on and drive this forward. You told me you wanted to do it. Then today you walked into my office with Christine, both looking like we'd asked you to pack cakes for a living and with about as much energy as a dead rabbit."

I briefly wondered whether to ask him where packing cakes and dead rabbits had come from, but luckily he just carried on.

"You are supposed to be the one leading this. Much as we know it's important and want to see it work, we do have other things to worry about as well. You have to be the one causing us all to change. If you've already lost interest, then we'll either have to abandon the whole thing or find someone else to do it. And I don't think we are going to abandon it, if you get my drift."

I told him that, yes, I got his drift, and then confided in him what had happened between Christine and me before the meeting.

"Good."

"Why is it good? I think we need Christine to make the new strategy work."

"Because she cares and there's something she would die in the ditch over – which is vital for anyone involved in strategy. So let's make sure she stays. What would you die in the ditch over?"

He will have noticed me deal with this question by immediately looking down at the table. I caught myself doing it too late to stop. I breathed out, nodded and then looked him in the eyes. I really had nothing to say. He knew that I had accepted his challenge but had no immediate answer.

He carried on.

"The problem has always been that you folks in IT make promises that you then don't keep. So either you're over-promising in the first case, struggling with execution, or both. If you propose a strategy, and we all agree with it, then we expect you to get a buzz from achieving it and die in the ditch over it just like the rest of us have to. Have you noticed how passionate Juliette is about strategy? She finds it a real turn-on, gets visibly aroused. She knows that people - both men and women - notice and doesn't care. She just hopes some of it will rub off on others. I react differently, but I'm no less passionate. The only time I've seen you show any real passion is when I told you James was in on this, too. Goodness knows why that should bother you." He paused, but not long enough for an answer. "Look, I'm my strategy, James is his and Juliette hers. We know where our strategies converge and where they diverge. The strategic energy is in the differences more than the overlaps. You guys go on all the time about business-IT alignment as if it is some binary thing. You don't seem to have noticed that we business people and our strategies are not fully aligned with each other. It would be too risky if we were. With no inter-strategy conflicts to challenge our tactics, we would all probably head over a cliff together like lemmings. So by Friday, please *be* your strategy and prepare yourself for the excitement of some tactical tensions and conflicts. Make a promise to Juliette, James and me that you are determined to keep, come what may, or don't make it. We can cancel the meeting, if you would prefer."

My gut reaction was to dispute whether I had kept my strategic promises. Hadn't we enabled the business to achieve the things we said they could? Was it my fault if they didn't achieve them? Hadn't we tried to push benefits realization, investment planning and project management but been thwarted by the company culture in our efforts to make things better? Before I had decided how much of this to voice, he carried on:

"I don't blame you for being upset."

"I'm not upset...."

"Your whole industry is renowned for making bold promises and then not keeping them. You've got yourself caught up in the industry culture. We want you to break loose, join the gang, help us turn the tables on those bastards in IT and make sure we do something even bigger and better for ourselves at the same time."

"But I am one of those bastards in IT, as you call them."

"Only the other day you were denying it. Well stay there if you want, but not with us."

He was whispering now as we were still in the restaurant, and could be seen and possibly overheard.

"What are you saying, Graham? That I take on your new strategy or that's it? Why can't I carry on being the CIO like I am now?"

"Because we don't need anyone in your role any more. We think that, all in all, our people out there now know enough about IT and how to use it not to need an executive to make those decisions for us. All we really need is someone who can source the IT services we want to use, delivered at the right kind of price and risk, and with economies of scale and synergies where possible. I think you call that a Chief Technology Officer. I expect he or she will work for Frank in Procurement. Why should procuring and managing IT products and services be such a special case? We are also going to absorb everything else you have been calling IT into our mainstream business management, wherever it belongs, so we can make sure that being an expert customer of IT suppliers is embedded into our management DNA."

"When did you decide that?"

"Juliette and I discussed it yesterday. Sounds like you're off the pace, old boy."

"Christine will be working for me, though, won't she." Half a statement, half a question.

"No. Christine is going to work with James."

"But I thought Christine would be working for me," starting to repeat myself.

"Why? Setting the standards for business planning and making sure we all manage the finances properly is at the heart of James's accountabilities. One of the main reasons that Christine and Harry failed to make it stick before was because the initiative was coming from you, from IT. You should have made sure it was coming from Finance."

"Harry's from Finance, and anyway Martin overreacted and scared everyone."

"But Harry was clearly acting as Christine's helper, not the other way around. And I didn't hear anything in your story about challenging Martin, if you thought he was wrong."

I asked him if we could go somewhere else – somewhere private - to continue our conversation.

"There's hardly anybody left here – look – but we can go to my office if you would prefer."

I looked around and saw that he was right. There was hardly anyone left and I hadn't noticed. I said that I still would prefer to go to his office, so we did.

"So what about the other things we do?" I asked.

"Go on."

"Business Analysis. Enterprise Architecture. Project Delivery. Market Research."

"Christ, how many different things are you people trying to do? No wondering you're struggling. Anyway, if those are things we need to be doing as core competencies, we'll integrate them where they belong. If not, we'll just regard them as services we can buy and the CTO can decide whether to keep them in-house or buy them from a supplier. To use the model you and Christine were working on the other day, they're either We or Not We. So if Project Delivery is just about deploying technology, then it's a service that the CTO can have in his team or buy when we need it. If it's about delivering the benefits of our investments, then maybe it should stay with you or go to work directly for project sponsors. I'm not sure about Enterprise Architecture. What's that all about?"

"It's the people who do what we currently call Strategy."

"Simon?"

"That's right"

"What do they 'architect', as you call it?"

"Business processes, information, systems, technologies."

"That's not enterprise, that's capital." He saw my blank look. "Factors of Production. Economics."

"Economics or not, it's what everyone calls Enterprise Architecture."

He seemed to accept this retort, at least for the time being.

"Well, if it's a core competency, we'll integrate that, and Business Analysis, into my own strategy group and learn where they fit. As I mentioned the other day, James also has some financial business analysts, so it's possible some of yours might go to him. "

"I don't expect so. I'm sure they would be a better fit with you." Changing the subject back to the CTO, I then said, "I don't think Purchasing really understands sourcing, let alone sourcing IT."

"Speaking frankly, no pun intended, you could be right. Frank and his team may well need to take more accountability for the day-to-day operational consequences of the sourcing decisions they make and the contracts they negotiate. If so, then we'll use the integration of IT into Procurement to highlight the issue and resolve it."

"This is a very different model. I can see the logic from your perspective, but I'm struggling to see how it will work."

Graham looked me in the eye and after a short pause, nodded slightly and drew a breath.

"Look," he said "I think we've nearly finished for now. Do you have any questions?"

"If Christine is going to work for James, who is going to work for me?"

"That's one of the things we need you to say. My hunch is that you'll need a new team who know about driving people to deliver a return on a portfolio of investments. They will probably know something about our kind of business and maybe about creating value by exploiting IT. It may be better that way round than IT people who think they know something about investments."

"What about my operational contribution to the company? I don't think people will take me seriously unless I have one."

"Investment management will be your operational contribution. It's not some kind of ivory-tower thing. It may not be the same as running one of our business units or delivering IT, but it's still operational in its own context. Don't tell the investment guys in the City of London or over on Wall Street that what they're doing is not operational, as well as strategic. They work extremely hard."

"OK. But I still don't understand what the difference is between what you're asking me to do and Finance."

"Well, that's like asking why Finance doesn't run all our business units, which are also about delivering a return on investment, when you get down to basics. It would give James and our finance people a deep conflict of interests. Your team may well have to drive Finance to do things differently, in ways they might not want to, and vice versa."

"How does James feel about that?"

"It's a real shame you're asking me that and not him."

Observations

- The strategist has to cause other people to change.
- Know what you would 'die in the ditch' over.
- The corporate strategists' perspectives of IT: not keeping promises and not caring enough about strategy?
- The strategic energy is in the conflicts. 100% alignment between strategies is unlikely and potentially disastrous.
- The future value of the CIO role is not assured.
- There are competencies in IT departments that also exist elsewhere in a company.
- A new generation of strategy for IT requires a different operating model.

EIGHTEEN

M	T	W	T	F	S	S	M	T	W	T	F
									▌		✕

Graham's comment about me asking him what James felt effectively concluded our discussion, as I didn't really have a response and he had to move on to another meeting. I went back to the empty restaurant and sat on the sofa Christine and I had been using all along and stared out of the window. The sun was not setting, it was too early in the day, but it seemed like it should have been.

A hand touched me gently on the shoulder. I turned around and it was Christine. She had made it as far as the railway station to catch the train to Windsor and decided to come back. Graham's PA had told her that we had finished our meeting and Christine had guessed where to find me.

"I'm sorry about earlier, Ian." she said as she sat down next to me.

"That's OK. Actually, in a perverse way it helped enormously. Things are becoming clearer by the minute."

"I'm going to end up working for James, aren't I?"

"Yes."

"How do you feel about that?"

"I'd rather you were still going to work for me, but I think I can see the logic. How do you feel?"

"Not sure – is he OK? To work for, I mean?"

"Yes, I think he is. For a CFO, he's actually quite nice. Only joking." Joking, but not smiling

"What about the rest of us, who will they end up working for?"

"That's for me to decide, at least in principle." I lied, "But it sounds like Juliette and Graham already have some ideas."

"I think all this is right, Ian."

"Why?"

"Because the whole IT thing needs a big shake up – not just here, everywhere. It seems to be in a cul-de-sac of our own making. The only way to make it progress much further is with a radical rethink, some significant innovation. I just wish we'd thought of it before they did."

"I think we've known what the problem is for some time. At least some of us have. We've been too narrow in thinking strategically about how to solve it and probably been hoping to play it safe. I suppose it was only a question of time before the real corporate strategists decided to wade in."

"And now it has happened, well, in this company anyway, I don't expect the picture will ever be the same again."

"No, it won't. They will make it work differently. They only deal in success."

"They?"

"Juliette and Graham. James. Marianne."

"What about you, Ian? What about me?"

"Are you one of them now? Have you decided?"

"Actually, no, I'm one of us. I'm in. It sounds like you aren't. Is that it, are you going to turn us down?"

"No. I am going to do it. I have a day and a bit to finally cross the bridge from supplier to customer, become a corporate strategist, make my promise and then keep it."

"Thank goodness for that. What can I do to help?"

"Nothing, thanks. Just go and see James tomorrow and make sure the investment planning works this time."

"Right, boss. Will do. See you around."

She started to stand up.

"Christine."

"Yes, Ian."

"Thanks for coming back."

"That's OK."

With that, she leaned over and kissed me, and left.

Observations

- Strategists deal only in success.
- It can be hard for incumbents to challenge the orthodoxies.
- A customer's strategy for exploiting IT has to be led by one of the customer's corporate strategists.
- If the CIO is reluctant to 'cross the bridge' from quasi-supplier to fully-fledged corporate strategist then leadership of any corporate strategy for IT will be vested in someone else.

NINETEEN

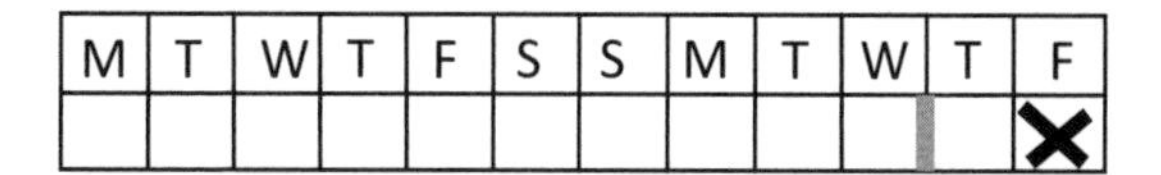

I didn't sleep well that night. I don't think I have ever felt so alone. The situation seemed quite bizarre – everyone wanted to help, but so far they had all walked away. Is this what strategy is really like, at its heart? Just one man or woman, with a promise to make and keep, a mountain to climb and goodness knows how many unexpected pitfalls and hazards to deal with? I had understood strategy to be a team game, all-conquering with a clear plan of attack. Or a seventy-eight page document making statements of genuine intent but that nobody really held anyone accountable for. I was also bemused why someone like Juliette would find strategy such a turn-on and expect others to feel the same?

Maybe it was the sense of influence over events that a real strategy gives people. That they can deal with whatever happens, steer things whenever they can, towards the promise they've set themselves. Harnessing the vagaries of the world, of fate and of the people they come into contact with just enough to achieve something extraordinary or even momentous.

Like solving, once and for all, the fundamental strategic problems that companies have had with IT.

It's true that I had always been comfortable writing strategies that I knew we might not really be able to achieve, knowing that we would be forgiven either explicitly or tacitly for not achieving them.

Or not, in the case of Juliette and her inner circle. This time, they were offering me a different choice: promise something meaningful, momentous but achievable, walk into the spotlight, and win.

Win and become a corporate strategist. Or not, and go somewhere else.

Observations

- Leading strategy can be a lonely job.
- Strategies are about winning: a strategy that you're not fully committed to achieving is not really a strategy.

TWENTY

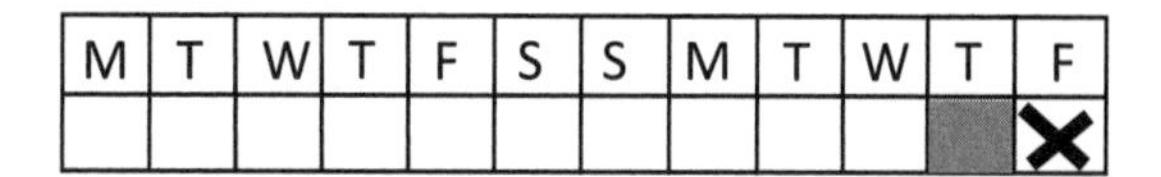

M	T	W	T	F	S	S	M	T	W	T	F
											X

I spent all of Thursday working on the strategy and ended up printing it on a single side of paper. I reckoned that I could explain the rest if people wanted me to, either to help them decide whether it was the right strategy or to understand in more detail how we were going to execute it. Christine sent me the team's final best shot at the numbers early in the afternoon with some notes as to what they did, and didn't, appear to tell us. In terms of the overall picture they painted, there was nothing materially different from the earlier version. Having read their notes, I concluded the main things worth exploring with Juliette and my other executive colleagues and finalized a set of notes of my own. I also pondered Justin's guidance to choose a number for the strategy to be all about and that I wanted to be accountable for. As he predicted, it wasn't the IT budget.

By the end of Thursday, concluding an extraordinary few days' experiences, I was scared, angry, excited and determined. I had committed myself to staying and winning, concluded what I thought we all needed to do, and had, at last, become the strategy.

I expect you're curious what I said on my one side of paper and what I decided to say about the numbers. Looking at it now, it seems blindingly obvious to me. To some, it seemed like that at the time, too. That was one of the reasons it worked. It was only obvious once someone had thought it through and written it down.

If I had not gone through the experiences that I did, though, between those two Thursdays, it would never have worked. I would not have understood what I needed to understand about the need for me, or someone else, to 'be' the strategy. The object lesson was shockingly simple: the strategy is not what you write down, it is who you are, what you actually do and what you influence others to do. Nowadays, I look at what someone really does with their time and the decisions they make to find out what their strategy is. When what they do, and decide, are different from whatever they have written, I ignore that part of whatever they wrote. In some cases, a person's 'de facto' strategy is almost perfectly the opposite of the one they wrote down.

For the record then, here is my strategy paper as it stood on that Thursday evening and as I presented to Juliette, Graham and James on that Friday. You have already seen earlier versions of the thinking that went into it, so bear with me if I appear to be repeating myself. Anyway, you should see some material changes:

Summary

This is our corporate strategy for exploiting Information Technologies (IT). In formulating it, we have pinpointed the fundamental cause of our main strategic issue with IT – the delivery of real business value – and what we all need to do about it. In essence, we are turning traditional IT strategy on its head. Instead of starting with IT and trying to deliver and measure business value, we are going to start with how we create and measure value and work backwards. The issue we associate with IT is not really about IT at all, but our ability and determination to create value from our investments in change – whether or not those investments involve IT. Our overall strategy for resolving this issue is first to deal with our investments involving IT, and then apply what we learn to all our other investments. We are entering the end game in our corporate strategy for IT. When we have finished, our strategy for IT will be not to have one.

Strategy Promise (outcome)

We will maximize the value we create for customers and investors from all our investments involving IT.

Key Principles (truths)

- Our strategies and business plans depend, in part, on us successfully exploiting IT.
- IT on its own delivers no value.
- "Value" is a portfolio of measures and is whatever our company's strategies and operating plans say that it is.
- The future costs of IT to P&L and cash are important numbers for us to manage because of the business decisions that cause them.
- Each director is accountable for the value their part of the company creates from investments involving IT.
- The CIIO (see below) is accountable for the total value that the company creates from all our new investments in changes involving IT.

Core Tactics (actions)

- Plan and execute our investments in business changes by starting with value creation and working backwards.

- Focus our investments in business changes involving IT on those types of value that are vital to our strategies and where we can exploit IT to make the highest contribution.
- Kill off the IT investment plan and IT budget as standalone entities.
- At business unit and corporate levels, proactively manage the total impact of business change projects on IT costs to P&L and cash.
- Integrate 'expert IT customer' competencies where they belong in our company management structure.
- Replace the Chief Information Officer (CIO) with a Chief Internal Investments Officer (CIIO).
- Appoint experienced investment managers and project managers who specialize in benefits delivery.
- Reward project managers based on the measurable value we achieve from their projects.
- Use media coverage of this strategy to enhance investor appreciation of our value creation credentials.

And that was it. My biggest worry was that I had written too little and that it all seemed so obvious.

As an appendix to the strategy paper, I also provided the spreadsheets that Christine, Barry and Lawrence had worked so hard to compile and summarized what I thought we had so far learned from that process. This was also very different for me, as I had always before provided pictures - such as architectural diagrams, Gantt-chart type project plans, organization charts - not numbers, as the main supporting documents for strategy. Graham later told me that he had been encouraging me to paint pictures with the numbers. Whenever Juliette had to brief the main Board on strategy, numbers were usually the main currency of conversation.

The main points I summarized in preparation for my voiceover were these:

- We had been applying some of the right principles and processes, but to the wrong numbers. The IT numbers were, in business terms, meaningless on their own. Random numbers, as Graham had said. They were just fragments of the business investments needed to create value, either from existing operations or within new projects. Yet we had been following industry dogma, totaling these random fragments of investment because they were for IT. When the IT total came to more than the company thought was reasonable we reprioritized the 'IT investments', not the total business investments of which they were part

- Along the same lines, I could now see that the process Christine and Harry had attempted with Martin's business unit had been flawed on two counts. It had fallen into that trap of just presenting the IT numbers and encouraged people to make decisions in isolation of the wider business numbers they were part of. Also, Christine and Barry had not offered the review group any options and recommendations for what to do with the numbers when they saw them. I think that if they had listed the option of cancelling all the projects that were out of line with the overall business priorities, Martin himself would have probably explained the danger in doing so.

- It wasn't entirely clear why we had ever separated out the projects that involved IT from all the other business projects and treated them as a special case. It had been going on for so long that maybe nobody could remember. Our strategy was, therefore, to build backwards to the position we should have been taking all along. First, by shifting the strategic focus for projects involving IT from the IT numbers to the overall business numbers; and then making it irrelevant whether or not a project involved IT.

- We were making no provision in our forward investment plans for investments that were not yet assigned to value types and projects. My intuition was that the process of assigning investment from a provision to a project was key to the execution of our strategy.
- The future costs of IT to P&L and cash did seem to be worth managing carefully. They might represent relatively small, random numbers in overall business terms, but I didn't think we should just let them float free. On the contrary, because of where these numbers came from - the causes and effects behind them - there were strategic advantages to managing them carefully, to influence business decisions, culture and behaviors. I reckoned this is what Juliette, and then Graham, had suddenly realized when she had briefly left our meeting a week earlier.

That's all I could think of saying, at a summary level. I had figured out the overall strategy and had some perspectives on what execution would look like. It would either work or it wouldn't, so I went home, relaxed and slept.

Observations

- Set down your Promise, Principles and Tactics for the key stakeholders to explore and ratify.
- They should see a synthesis of their individual perspectives as well as yours.
- A strategy may look like the obvious until people see - for example from the numbers - that they are not currently applying it in practice.
- Use your strategy to test the relevance of industry 'best practices'.
- Strategy is what you do and who you are: your 'de facto' strategy is your strategy.

TWENTY ONE

M	T	W	T	F	S	S	M	T	W	T	F
											X

Juliette called me early next morning while I was still at home, and asked me to drop by her office 15 minutes before the meeting, which I did.

"How many pages do you have for me this time?" she asked with a shard of humor in her eye.

"One. And the numbers as appendices. I've prepared to summarize verbally what I think they tell us."

"Wow. I'm impressed. What does the one page say?"

I handed over her copy of the strategy paper and the appendices. She scanned the paper, flicked to the numbers, briefly scanned them too and then turned back to the main page.

"This is fine, Ian," she said in a neutral voice. "I see you've made my first Principle into your second one."

"That's because the one I've now put first gives the second one a context, which it would otherwise lack."

"That's true. We'll need to see what the others think of the strategy, but I'm happy for you to propose it to us. Interesting numbers." What, I briefly wondered, would have happened if she had not had been happy? I would never know.

Once we had all sat down, Juliette opened the meeting and handed it straight over to me. I gave Graham and James their copies of my documents. All three quietly read my one-page strategy paper and looked through the numbers. I talked through the notes I had made. Then they just looked at each other for a few seconds. Juliette said later that they were deciding, having got me this far, whether they also had the courage to see this one through and whether I was the right person for the job. They knew each other well enough that they did not always have to discuss things out loud.

Satisfied with the non-verbal signals from Graham and James, Juliette spoke first. "This looks great, Ian." Juliette said. "Are you sure you want to do it?"

"Yes, I am."

"Good."

Graham smiled slightly, although he dropped his head as if trying to hide it.

Juliette continued, "Gentlemen, do you have any questions you'd like Ian to answer?"

James spoke first. "There are some things I'd like to do with the structure of your spreadsheets. I should say first that I agree with the overall direction in which they are heading. I want to build on the work you've done, not unpick it. How do you feel about that?"

"I'm very pleased, James. If you'd said that three days ago, I would have felt defensive about whose spreadsheets these were. But today, the important thing for me is not the way we structure the numbers, but what the numbers are. I need to get us all understanding and managing the right numbers in the first place. With the relationship we already have, and with Christine working for you, I'm sure that we'll have no problem. If I need the numbers in a particular shape, then I'll tell you."

James put his elbows on the meeting table and loosely entwined his fingers.

Graham leaned forward slightly, suddenly looking me directly in the eyes and asked the next question.

"What if the strategy doesn't work?"

"It will. I expect some of our detailed tactics will turn out to be wrong, but the strategy will work."

"How do you know?"

I had to pause and consider this one.

"I don't think this is about knowing. It's about determination and belief."

"This isn't a job interview. That sounds like an interview answer."

"I know this isn't an interview, although my job here is still on the line. It wasn't an interview answer, simply what I believe."

"OK. Let me rephrase my question. What is it about your strategy that makes you believe it will win?"

"Two things. If the Principles are sound, then there's only so long that things can continue to go wrong when we all start to apply them – provided that we also keep reviewing our tactics in light of events. The Principles are, after all, basic truths. If they're not, then I need to think again. The other reason I believe the strategy will win is because I am going to make sure that it does. Do you agree with my Principles?"

"The one I'm not sure about is the last one – about the role you've called the CIIO. It's not necessarily true that such a role exists. However, assuming that it does then I do agree with the accountability you've given it. I also agree that we will only see the maximum value of all our internal investments when one person's accountable for delivering it. It's not an accountability that fits with any of the executive roles we currently have, so I also agree that it's a new role – whatever we might choose to call it. So yes, I agree with your Principles."

"Juliette, James, do you also agree with the strategy's Principles?"

James spoke next. "Yes, I do."

Then Juliette. "You know, they seem quite dangerous, because they're very different from the de facto principles we've all been applying to our IT decisions until now. The second one, that you told me about last week, says exactly the opposite of the way we have been behaving."

"What are you saying – do we need to water them down? I would find that hard to do."

"No, not that. It's not the fundamental Principles themselves, I suppose, more the impact of telling people what they are and applying them in practice." So Juliette's strategy brain was figuring out all the cultural and behavioral implications of making the Principles public and using them to influence what people did. She continued, "We have to balance our desire to tell people our strategy with the implications for its success if we do. My preference is to tell people, but there are times when we shouldn't."

"I'd like people to know what this strategy is. It will make it easier to explain why we're expecting them to do things differently."

"Yes, so would I. Here's what I think we should do. Ask Marianne to help you convey what you have written here for a different audience. Don't alter what it says, just adjust the way that we articulate it."

"Do you have a specific example that I can use to explain to Marianne what we think the issue is?"

"Take that second Principle. It is undoubtedly true, but potentially very controversial. Some people may simply object to what it says because of the way it's worded and take an opposing position, yet would agree with it if we expressed it differently. If people do fundamentally disagree with our strategic principles we want to know - we can help them to explore why and decide what they want to do. But that's not the same as unintentionally provoking a hostile reaction because of the way we've worded things. I don't know what the answer is, but I'd like you and Marianne to find a way of articulating the same truth, but in a way that's less likely to trigger an unhelpful response."

"Thank you, that's very helpful. I'd like to move on to the Tactics."

"Presumably these aren't everything we'll need to do," said James.

"These are the main tactical themes that I think will be the difference between success and failure."

"It's interesting that none of them are about technology."

"No, because if we get these things right, then I'm confident we'll be making the most appropriate technology decisions as we go along."

"What do you mean by 'integrating expert IT customer competencies' where they belong? Haven't you done that already with your IT/Business Partnerships people?"

"This is different because we have identified specific areas of competency and knowledge within the IT department that is the same as, or similar to, other areas of the company. Until now we've been cramming all sorts of different competencies into the IT department because they are about IT. Now we think it's time to integrate these with the other areas that primarily represent these competencies and can make best use of the related IT expertise."

"That all sounds plausible, but a bit abstract. Is Christine moving to my area a tangible example?"

"Yes."

"Thank you."

I looked around for other questions about my proposed tactics.

After a short silence, Juliette asked, "Does anyone have anything else you want Ian to answer or bear in mind?"

James again. "I'd just like to go back to your principles and tactics about the numbers. So the total amounts of P&L and cash we invest in IT are, to use your words, random numbers because they're assembled from varying-sized fragments of investment within business operations and projects. And they're not very big numbers in the grand scheme of things. But you're saying we should still worry about what those numbers are?"

"I don't think we need to be too concerned by the absolute numbers themselves, but I am recommending we use them as levers to drive changes in business behavior exactly because they are made up of fragments of the investment we make in so many different business activities. I also think we have to choose which IT number we're primarily going to use.

I'm recommending using the cost of IT to P&L because it offers us the most levers. Other options – such as IT capital, IT service costs or IT costs to cash – limit our scope to change behaviors because they don't offer so many levers."

"Thank you." James concluded.

Juliette asked, "Anything else?"

Graham and James shook their heads.

"Graham, will you continue to act as Ian's mentor while he still needs one?"

"Sure."

"Right. OK Ian, what's next?"

"I need to have that conversation with Marianne about language and communication as soon as I can – I'll call her immediately after we've finished."

"Good." Juliette agreed. "I'd like you to brief the full Executive Team at our monthly meeting next Wednesday. Provided that goes well, then we're off! Then, get us all together again as soon as possible to start addressing your second Tactic. I want you to drive the debate on the main types of value we want from our investments and the implications for our current investment plans."

"Will do. Finally, in terms of my own position, where do I stand? I'd like to be your Chief Internal investments Officer - CIIO - as my paper says, and have a full seat on the Executive team."

"To have that, you'll need to take primary accountability for a significant element of the company's financials, including the outcomes we generate from them." So Justin was spot-on. "The problem with the position you've held is that other people have always had ultimate accountability for the money you've been managing. Like you said, it's been a random number made up of fragments of business investment. Putting it bluntly, you've been spending other people's money with no accountability for the ultimate business outcomes, at the end of the day. No criticism of you intended, just a statement of the facts."

I cut in. "No offence taken. Here's what I propose, subject to backing from you and these gentlemen here, and depending on the reaction we get from the executives next week. I want you to hold me personally accountable for the total value we create from all the resources we invest in internal investment projects involving IT. In time, if it all works out, I would like you to remove the 'involving IT' limitation."

Juliette took over again. “OK. Apart from me, you have the final say in how we use both our financial and other resources for the portfolio of programs and projects that fall under your scope. I expect you will proactively seek the guidance, but not necessarily consensus, of a group of your executive peers including me. I will never go around you in cases of dispute. I will assign the financial resources to you directly. You will need to harness other resources, such as our people, with the consent and collaboration of the executives and managers who look after them. If we have material resources working on projects in your scope, but without your consent, I will hold you accountable. Graham and James, do you agree with what I am telling Ian?”

“Yes.”

“Yes.”

“So Ian, with all of that in mind, do you want to become my CIIO?”

“Yes.”

“Then as far as this group is concerned, you are now the CIIO. You’ll need to keep that confidential until at least next Wednesday. In fact, let’s use the Executive meeting to give you our official endorsement. If we’re all done, then?”

Juliette looked at each of us in turn. We were indeed all done, and the session finished. As I got up to leave, Juliette walked over and put her hand on my arm. It was gentle, but I could feel huge energy in the touch. "Well done Ian," she said, "I know we've a long way to go. I've been carefully restrained today, but I want you to know that I'm very, very excited about this."

And I could tell that she was, just as I was.

Observations

- If the company manages its investments well, the most appropriate technology decisions will follow.
- At an early stage, facilitate an agreement among the executives - using a value portfolio - on the strategic priorities for investments in change while also considering the consequences for the current investment plans.
- Assign executive accountability for maximizing the total value the company creates from internal investments in change.

TWENTY TWO

Aftermath

The early part of the following week, leading up to the Executive meeting on Wednesday, was surreal. I found it frustrating not being able to tell anyone the world-changing events of the previous Friday, and could only start executing the outcome in my head. Internally, I was a very different person, but externally I was bound to keep everything the same.

Christine phoned me as soon as she thought the Friday meeting was finished. All I could tell her, with no intonation one way or another, was that we had reached a consensus on the way forward, that it was subject to a full Executive meeting on Wednesday and I would be in a position to let her and others know what this meant towards the end of the following week. Meanwhile, she was to be very discreet about the conversations with Juliette, Graham, James and Marianne and I knew that I could trust her to do so. Barry also phoned me on Saturday, apologizing for not doing so on Friday due to other pressing commitments. I told him the same as I had said to Christine.

I noticed that Simon didn't contact me. By Tuesday, however, either I was becoming paranoid or I was getting odd looks from people close to him whenever I passed them in the office. Time would tell.

The Wednesday Executive meeting was a success. Each of the directors appeared either enthusiastic or neutral, and there were no dissenting voices to my new title and accountabilities. Those members of the Executive group who were Managing Directors of businesses were especially concerned about how we were going to distinguish the time that their people spent on projects from that spent on day-to-day operations and whether it would turn into an unwelcome 'cottage industry' of form-filling, reporting and control. They seemed reassured to hear that none of us would be happy if that happened and by my view that most people would normally be on either projects or day-to-day operations, so we were probably talking about relatively few people who were routinely on both. I told them that if they didn't see the benefits of doing this, then we would need to consider whether we were approaching it the right way.

Juliette asked the group what they thought the major constraints would be on the strategy's execution. By then, I had learned enough about strategists from her, Graham and Justin in particular, to know that she was often asking two questions at once. By answering the prima-facia question, executives were indeed highlighting those things that would make the execution of the strategy difficult, given the environment in which it was to succeed. The main constraints they talked about were: people's understanding of what this new strategy was all about; cultural inertia; the availability and retention of the few key people on whom most of our company's strategies seemed to depend; money; our ability to manage and execute change; the level of alignment between the company's other strategies. Interestingly, nobody mentioned technology as a major constraint, although some of the key people that our strategies depended on did work in my (former) IT department.

The executives' answers to Juliette's question about constraints also answered her other reason for asking it. The executives had also told me, her and Graham what levers to focus on to successfully execute the strategy. She didn't keep any of this a secret – she immediately echoed the constraints back to the other executives and asked them if these also represented the main levers of execution for the strategy to focus on, which they confirmed to be so.

Juliette's philosophy was that scarcity, not abundance, drives strategy. Strategy provides the context for choices and scarcity drives us to make them. So constraints are opportunities.

The Wednesday meeting voted to make me the new CIIO. Juliette released an email to all staff and a press release targeted at investors within an hour of the end of the meeting. A good sign that we were innovating was that news agencies very quickly started phoning our communications office for clarification of what the changes meant: what was a CIIO? The reception from the investor community was cautious, but fairly warm (since the whole point of my new role was to manage their stakes in the company even more rigorously).

As soon as Juliette's email hit people's Inboxes, I could sense the energy it created. Christine and Barry were back on the telephone to congratulate me and to start confirming what the changes meant for them and their people. We quickly booked a theatre in Windsor to brief everyone in the IT department on what was to happen. Most of the people we were planning to integrate into the wider company – IT business analysts, enterprise architects, IT service managers, Christine's team, and Barry's – were en masse tentatively positive, if apprehensive. It left me pondering how much they had already perceived the problems we had built up by having 'IT' as a separate entity from 'the business' and trying to do a bit of everything. Later, once we had made the changes and integrated all the IT specialists where they best belonged, there weren't many people who expressed nostalgia for the good old days in IT.

In between the email announcement and the theatre briefing, Simon asked for a private conversation with me about the changes. I realized that I had been paying him less credit as my Strategy Manager than I perhaps ought to have done during the time that I had been formulating the new strategy. With hindsight, out of respect for him and his role, maybe I should have briefed him privately at least once or twice on events as they were unfolding. But on the other hand, I don't think he would have been able to keep it to himself. Historically, he had demonstrated a tendency to quietly whip up support against developments that he didn't personally agree with.

We met around the corner from our London office, in Kimberley's coffee shop. She was still as cheery as always, but in her eyes I could see that she was registering our seriousness and simply served us our coffees with a smile.

"I think this new strategy is all wrong," Simon started.

"Please can you tell me why?"

"This isn't an IT Strategy. In fact, I don't think it's really a strategy at all."

"On your first point, I agree. It definitely isn't an IT Strategy. At the risk of being patronizing, it even says so. It's our Corporate Strategy for Exploiting IT. As for it not being a strategy, you would need to have that argument with Juliette and Graham. They've been guiding me on this from the very start."

"But you and I know it's not really about IT, is it? We're being used as a scapegoat for other people's problems."

I decided to ignore his blatant attempt, in his first sentence, to wrap us both into his personal views. There were bigger fish to fry. "I'm afraid it's the other way around, Simon. We've been rescuing some people from poor or incomplete business decisions and acting as their scapegoat. Now we've stopped. Instead, we're integrating ourselves with the other people in our company and the things they are planning to achieve, to make the best contribution we can."

"You're wrong, Ian."

This was rare, for Simon to be so direct with me – although I knew he was sometimes this way with others.

"This isn't a question of being right or wrong, Simon. Juliette and the executives have decided what they would now like us to contribute to the success of the company. I've taken their feedback that traditional

IT Strategies no longer do it for them, if indeed our strategies ever did. If we'd listened more carefully to Christine and Barry at our workshop a few weeks ago, we could have done something differently ourselves. When we produce the best IT Strategy we can, which passes our own industry's Best Practice benchmarks with flying colors, but the CEO asks 'what the hell she is supposed to do with this', to quote Juliette directly, I've taken it on the chin that it's time to change. So I agree with you that the new Corporate Strategy for Exploiting IT is nothing like a traditional IT Strategy. But our company executives prefer their new strategy and want us to lead them in executing it. We need to forget about 'right' and 'wrong' and focus, instead, on the opportunities and choices we are being offered. It took me quite a few days to understand what I was being offered and make the choice. I strongly recommend you also take a few days to think it through."

"Too late! I'm leaving. I've got another job. How soon can I go?"

"I'm sorry that you've decided so quickly. I think we are moving on to a whole new generation of strategy for IT and it's a shame you don't want to be part of it. However, I can see that it doesn't fit with what you come to work for in the morning. How soon do you want to go?"

"Right now, actually."

"OK. Let me talk to Human Resources and we'll see how quickly we can release you. I can't promise when that will be, but I'll make it as soon as we can."

That's how our conversation ended. I spoke to Karen, our HR Manager for IT, and felt the best thing to do was to let Simon go there and then. The risk of him trying to undermine the strategy was material and although we would have been able to turn this to the strategy's advantage, we saw no point in him coming in to work for us when he was so adamantly opposed to what we were doing. It seemed in nobody's interests. So I told him he could work out his three months' notice on 'gardening leave' and wished him luck in his new job.

For my part, I was relieved to give up managing IT delivery and the IT department to concentrate on leading the execution of the strategy. Despite having partly valued myself based on having a significant department to run, I had no regrets. I think I was bored with managing a traditional IT operation anyway.

For my new core team, we recruited five highly experienced investment managers from a number of different financial institutions - people who wanted a 'soft' career landing after years in the rat-race. We also brought in some of the IT Business Analysts and helped them grow their skills in investment analysis and portfolio management. The others went to work for Graham and thrived. For my part, I was shocked to find out how far we were behind orthodox investment thinking in managing our portfolio of internal investments. One of the people I hired mentioned 1952 to me shortly after joining, which meant nothing. So he told me about Harry Markowitz and Modern Portfolio Theory. I'm not qualified to tell you what that is all about, but I do now understand the basic principles and what they mean in practice for internal investments. If you're interested, I'd encourage you to look it up.

Christine worked for James as our Head of Investment Planning and improved on her earlier attempts at framing the investment plans. She didn't radically change any of the templates, just the depth and dimensions of the numbers we were working with and the end-to-end investment process. More importantly, she made the plans for investing in change integral to our business planning cycle and one of the main driving forces behind it.

We appointed Mark, my Technical Services Manager, as CTO reporting to Frank, widening Frank's own role from procurement to sourcing, including accountability for the day-to-day performance of our suppliers and their services. The CTO's role was to get the IT we wanted to use delivered reliably well, economically, at an acceptable level of risk, and with economies of scale and synergies. Nothing else.

Graham absorbed into his team those Enterprise Architects that were focused more on business architecture than technology. Accountability for shaping the technology architecture we used stayed with the CTO. One of the first things that Graham did with his new Enterprise Architects was to get them architecting 'enterprise' as defined by economics, rather than just 'capital'. He wanted them working on people's ideas and motivations for creating maximum value from the capital we were investing in, as well as helping to shape that capital. That turned out to be a major cultural factor in our strategy's success.

Barry and his project managers transferred to the Chief Operating Officer, putting accountability for on-the-ground changes in the hands of the people who ran the operations that needed changing.

Because change is not something you can easily do to someone. They really have to do it to themselves.

EPILOGUE

What, I sometimes wonder to this day, would have happened if I had made Simon write down the things that Christine and Barry had said in our workshop?

There's a side of me that believes, perhaps optimistically, that we could have come to a similar conclusion to Juliette and Graham. After all, we had five days and they only needed a few minutes. Or at least we might have gotten half way there and been better prepared for what followed.

On the other hand, we might not have triggered Juliette to reject the IT Strategy and start again if we had not produced it, or something like it. As a wise person once observed to me, sometimes the reason for producing something is so "at least we know that's wrong". So maybe we did exactly what was needed.

Who knows?

Juliette's inspiration, and innovation, was to use the idea of a strategy for IT to achieve something much more valuable than a traditional IT Strategy ever could. The one-piece-of-paper strategy for exploiting IT that she, Graham, Marianne and James helped me to formulate broke the mould in ways that were beyond my education and experiences and those of my IT team.

It also turned out to be the last 'IT strategy' that the company ever had. As we widened the scope of our 'internal investments' strategy to embrace projects that didn't involve IT, the residual Promise of the corporate strategy for IT became 'not to have one' which, if you follow me, is not the same as having no strategy.

A couple of years after the events I've described, when we had sorted out Juliette and her crew and made the CIIO a 'business as usual' role, a number of us moved onto our next company to team up with the CEO, CFO and the rest of the executive group and do it all again. We got better at it every time.

Ian Taylor
London, England
February, 2008